# Analytical Grammar

**Level 4**
**Phrases and Clauses**
Instructor Handbook

**Created by R. Robin Finley**

## ANALYTICAL GRAMMAR.

888-854-6284
analyticalgrammar.com
customerservice@demmelearning.com

**Analytical Grammar: Level 4, Phrases and Clauses Instructor Handbook**
© 1996 R. Robin Finley
© 2022 Demme Learning, Inc.
Published and distributed by Demme Learning

**analyticalgrammar.com**

1-888-854-6284 or 1-717-283-1448 | demmelearning.com
Lancaster, Pennsylvania USA

ISBN 978-1-60826-659-3
Revision Code 1122

Printed in the United States of America by CJK Group
  2 3 4 5 6 7 8 9 10

For information regarding CPSIA on this printed material call: 1-888-854-6284
and provide reference # 1122-11012022

# Table of Contents

# Level 4 | Phrases and Clauses

# Why We Learn Grammar

Children begin learning the grammar of their native language long before they can speak it fluently. Even a toddler knows that "Dad ate pizza" makes sense, while "Pizza ate dad" is silly! Unlike other subjects, we already know the grammar of our daily language—even if we don't know that we know it. The key, therefore, is two-fold:

- Apply labels to the different parts of speech and grammar. We know grammar; we just may not know the names of things or why they are organized in certain ways.

- Understand how to use different language and grammar in different situations. While formal situations call for more formal language, the grammar of our everyday, informal language is not incorrect. Correct grammar changes depending on the situation. Just as a person using informal slang might be judged in a formal business setting, the opposite is true: using formal language in an environment where casual language is the norm would seem strange.

These two components combine to make us better writers and, therefore, better communicators. Consistent use of grammar and proper use of punctuation helps keep written information flowing easily to the reader. With a mature understanding of grammar, students are better able to share their increasingly complex thoughts and ideas in a clear, understandable way.

## Getting Started

Some grammar "rules" are unbreakable. A sentence must always have a subject and a verb, for example. However, in many cases, rather than "rules," they should be looked at as "guidelines." Even professional grammarians (We do exist!) disagree on things like what a prepositional phrase is modifying in a sentence. Sometimes we even disagree with ourselves from day to day! This is okay. A sentence can be grammatically correct even if there is disagreement about how it is parsed or diagrammed. If your student has enough grammar knowledge to make an informed argument as to why they believe a certain answer is correct, it's a win—give them credit and move on.

The goal of each lesson is that students acquire enough familiarity with the topic that they can achieve 80% on the assessment. *Analytical Grammar* is intended to be an open-book curriculum, meaning that students are encouraged to use the lesson notes to complete all exercises and assessments, so this should not be a difficult goal if students are completing the exercises. Once a level is completed, the lesson notes and Application & Enrichment pages are designed to be removed from the book to create a grammar handbook that the student can use for life.

Grammar is a cumulative process. While new parts of speech will be addressed in subsequent lessons, students will continue to practice what they have already learned, and new skills will build upon that knowledge.

*Analytical Grammar* is just one component of a complete language arts program, which should include literature, writing, and vocabulary or spelling. By dividing the program into five levels, students are able to spend a short time focusing on grammar, then concentrate more fully on another component armed with the skills to improve their communication. Completing a reinforcement activity every couple of weeks and using the review lesson, when available, prior to starting the next level ensures that students' skills stay sharp.

### Components

Analytical Grammar is separated into five levels

**Level 1: Grammar Basics:** elementary introduction to the nine parts of speech.

**Level 2: Mechanics:** elementary guidelines for punctuation and word usage.

**Level 3: Parts of Speech:** complex information about parts of speech and their interactions

**Level 4: Phrases and Clauses:** advanced work with more complex components

**Level 5: Punctuation and Usage:** in-depth information about punctuation and word usage

For each level, you will need these components:

### Student Worktext

- *Student Notes* provide instruction and examples for each topic
- *Exercises A, B, and C* give students plenty of practice in applying their new knowledge
- *Application & Enrichment* activities provide weekly instruction and practice with functional writing skills
- *Assessments* are always open book and provide an accurate measure of proficiency
- *Reinforcement* worksheets are provided to keep skills sharp between levels

### Instructor's Handbook

- Page-by-page Student Worktext copy with solutions for all student work
- Instructor tips with additional explanation on possible points of confusion
- Item-by-item scoring guide for all assessments

**26-Week Schedule**

The study of grammar is just one part of a complete language arts program. Your student is expected to progress through the Analytical Grammar lessons at their own pace, then continue to practice grammar skills while studying another area of Language Arts.

## Review

| | |
|---|---|
| **Week 1** | Review |

## Lessons

| | |
|---|---|
| **Week 2** | Lesson 1 |
| **Week 3** | Lesson 2 |
| **Week 4** | Lesson 3 |
| **Week 5** | Lesson 4 |
| **Week 6** | Lesson 5 |
| **Week 7** | Lesson 6 |
| **Week 8** | Lesson 7 |

## Reinforcement

| | |
|---|---|
| **Week 9** | Break |
| **Week 10** | Exercise 1 |
| **Week 11** | Break |
| **Week 12** | Exercise 2 |
| **Week 13** | Break |
| **Week 14** | Exercise 3 |
| **Week 15** | Break |
| **Week 16** | Exercise 4 |
| **Week 17** | Break |
| **Week 18** | Exercise 5 |
| **Week 19** | Break |
| **Week 20** | Exercise 6 |
| **Week 21** | Break |
| **Week 22** | Exercise 7 |
| **Week 23** | Break |
| **Week 24** | Exercise 8 |
| **Week 25** | Break |
| **Week 26** | Exercise 9 |
| **Week 25** | Break |
| **Week 26** | Exercise 10 |

### An *Analytical Grammar* Week

Most *Analytical Grammar* lessons are set up in the same manner: a page of notes, three exercises, an Application and Enrichment activity, and an assessment. The following is a suggested schedule for completing one lesson a week.

## Monday

**Read over the lesson notes** with your student.

Have your student **complete Exercise A**.

- Work the first one or two sentences together, then have your student complete the rest. Remind them that they can use the lesson notes as needed throughout the week. Encourage them to ask for as much help as they need.

## Tuesday

**Review Exercise A.**

This should take no more than 20 minutes.

Discuss only those mistakes that relate to the lesson you are working on.

- For example, if you are working on a lesson focused on nouns, articles, and adjectives, just look at the words that are supposed to be marked. If your student has marked a verb as a noun, you can safely ignore it. These kinds of mistakes will correct themselves as students go through the program.

Have your student **complete Exercise B**.

## Wednesday

**Review Exercise B.**

Have your student **complete Exercise C**.

## Thursday

**Review Exercise C.**

**Read over and discuss the Application & Enrichment activity.**

Have your student **complete the Application & Enrichment activity**.

- Note that Application & Enrichment activities include important concepts for grammar proficiency, so don't skip them.

## Friday

**Review the Application & Enrichment activity.**

Have your student **complete the assessment**.

- Remind them that it is open book and they should use the lesson notes as much as necessary.

## The following Monday

**Correct the assessment** together.

- You read out the answers as your student crosses out any incorrect answers.

- Then, using the scoring guide found in the Instructor's Handbook on the assessment key, total up the correct answers and record the score on the test.

Now, **introduce the next lesson** and start the process all over again!

## Potential Activities

### Parsing

There are only nine parts of speech. Some parts will always have the same job in a sentence. Others can fill a variety of roles depending on how they are used. Identifying the parts of speech helps to narrow down the roles they may play. You will never find an adjective acting as an object, for example. Adjectives are always modifiers. On the other hand, nouns can do many different jobs in a sentence. Identifying parts of speech is called parsing. This is the first step to identifying the job that a word is doing in a sentence, since it helps students narrow down the possibilities.

art    adj    adj    n    av    pp    art    n    pp    art    n

**Example:**   The  quick  brown  fox  jumped  (over  the  dog)  (in  the  road).

### Short Answers and Fill-in-the-Blanks

Some exercises include short answer and fill-in-the-blank questions. These include activities like providing definitions, identifying a word's job in a sentence, and revising sentences to have proper punctuation.

### Diagramming and "The Process"

Diagramming a sentence can strike fear into even the most experienced grammar student. That's why we break it down into an easy-to-follow series of questions that we call "The Process." In small increments, by answering yes/no questions about the sentence, students learn to diagram increasingly complex sentences until they are confidently creating elaborate diagrams. Your student will be well prepared for the challenge. Some students enjoy the satisfaction of putting all of the parts of a sentence into their proper places.

We don't, however, diagram just for the sake of it. Diagramming visually demonstrates the structure of a sentence. It can clarify a relationship between two parts of speech like no amount of words can. While it is important to practice each new skill learned, once a student can demonstrate confidence with the part of speech, diagramming can be reduced, and you may find that your student doesn't need to complete every sentence in every exercise. It is simply a tool to support understanding of the parts that make up a sentence's structure. By Level 5, when grammar concepts are secondary to punctuation rules and guidelines, diagramming is put aside, but the knowledge acquired remains.

## Application & Enrichment

On the fourth day of each lesson, students will complete an Application & Enrichment activity. These activities are based on grammar, punctuation, and writing skills. They aren't usually directly related to the topic of the lesson, but they cover important concepts that will benefit students as they develop their writing skills. These activities provide a break from the lesson content, allowing students' brains an opportunity to store the grammar information they are learning in long-term memory. While these activities are intended to be fun and informative, they introduce and practice important skills and should not be skipped.

## Assessment

On the fifth day of a lesson, students have an opportunity to show you and themselves what they have learned. They will be asked to complete exercises that are similar to the daily exercises. Points are assigned to each section; they are found in the Instructor's Handbook with the solutions. The points are intended to be a measuring stick for how confident the student feels about the material. Remember, your student can use their lesson notes to complete the assessment. They should not try to complete it from memory, without support. Before moving to the next lesson, the goal is for your student to receive at least 80% on the assessment.If your student scores less than 80%, we recommend you review that lesson's notes with them before introducing the next topic and provide heavier support as they begin the new lesson's exercises.

## Notes on correcting assessments

When tallying assessment points, be sure to count the number correct. Don't count the number of errors and subtract that from the given number of total points. As your student acquires their grammar knowledge, they may mark a part of speech that shouldn't be marked in a particular lesson. Do not count these misplaced marks as incorrect. This problem will resolve itself in time as they progress through the program.

For assessments with diagrams, you will notice that the diagrams in the solutions have check marks indicating what should be counted as a "point." Go through your student's diagram item by item and compare the checked items. If an item is in the correct place, make a checkmark. If it's in the wrong place, circle it so that your student can see where they made a mistake.

For modifiers, if they are attached to the correct word and diagrammed correctly, count them as correct even if the word they are modifying is in the wrong place.

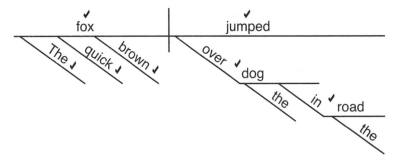

**Example:** The quick brown fox jumped (over the dog) (in the road).

This diagram is worth seven points. Points are assigned for the subject (fox), verb (jumped), fox's modifiers (The, quick, and brown), the prepositional phrase attached to "jumped" (over the dog), and the prepositional phrase attached to "dog" (in the road). Notice that although the prepositional phrases have three words, they each only have one check mark and therefore are worth one point as a unit.

Now imagine your student diagrammed the sentence like this:

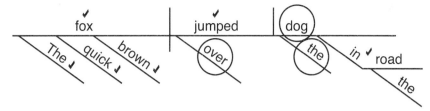

This diagram only loses one point. The prepositional phrase over the dog was only worth one point, so therefore it can only lose one point if it's incorrectly diagrammed. The prepositional phrase in the road is still correct and earns one point because it is correctly attached to *dog*.

### Reinforcement Exercises

The student worktext includes ten reinforcement exercises and answer keys that will keep your student's parsing, diagramming, and paraphrasing skills sharp. These exercises include material from a wide variety of books, poems, and stories. Students should complete, then correct, each exercise on their own. Assign one exercise every other week. If these skills are reinforced periodically, your student will be well-prepared when it's time to start Level 5.

## Tips for Success

This course can be adapted to meet your student's needs.

- If your student is confident, consider allowing them to "test out" of a lesson. Have them look over the lesson notes and, if they feel ready, take the lesson assessment. If the student scores at least 80% correct on the assessment, skip to the next lesson. They will still get plenty of practice with the skipped concept.

- If a lesson feels overwhelming and your student needs to slow down a little, have them do the odd sentences in an exercise one day and the evens the next.

- Consider only asking your student to diagram half of the sentences in an exercise. If they understand the concept and can identify the word, phrase, or clause that is the focus of the lesson, they do not necessarily need to diagram every sentence.

- On the other hand, encourage students to diagram at least one or two sentences from each lesson. Diagramming creates a visual image of how parts of speech interact. Allow them to choose which sentences they would like to diagram.

- Remind your student that they should look at the lesson notes for help as they are completing the exercises and even the assessment.

## Lesson 1
# Participial Phrases

### Instructor Notes

Now it's time to dig into more complex sentences. If you took any kind of break after completing *Analytical Grammar Level 3: Parts of Speech*, which includes the first ten lessons of *Analytical Grammar*, your student should complete the *Analytical Grammar: Parts of Speech* review lesson located at the beginning of the student worktext. Alternatively, review the lesson notes with your student and complete a few sentences from one of the worksheets for each lesson to be reviewed. Be sure that they remember how to parse and diagram using The Process Chart.

Students will find it valuable to complete the Verbals Chart for Lessons 1–3, found at the end of this lesson. This will help them keep track of the three easily confused kinds of verbals they are studying. They will be asked to complete the appropriate line of the chart before they begin the lesson exercises.

**Tip for Instructors**

If your student confidently completes Exercise A independently and without error, you may skip Exercises B and C and give them the option of taking the assessment early. If they score at least an 80% on the assessment, they are ready to move on. Decide with your student whether to jump into the next lesson immediately, or take a short break and wait for the following Monday. Either way, your student should still complete that lesson's Application & Enrichment activity before moving on.

# Lesson 1: Participial Phrases

By this point in the program, you have learned all of the parts of speech and many of their jobs. In Level 4, we will discuss parts of speech, phrases, and clauses that are doing jobs you might not expect. These uses add complexity and depth to your writing and allow you to move past short, simple sentences to talk about your ideas and opinions in a more mature and efficient way.

Do you remember seeing words that looked like verbs but didn't have a subject? We called them *verbals* and parsed them with **v**. While these words are all verbals, there are different kinds of verbals: participles, gerunds, and infinitives. We will learn about each of them in Lessons 1–3.

**Important:** Only verbs without subjects are verbals! If a verb has a subject, it is part of the verb phrase.

The first verbal we'll talk about is the *participle*.

### Participle

A participle is a verb form without a subject that acts like an adjective. There are two kinds of participles:

> **Present Participle:** a verb ending in "*-ing*" that will fit into the sentence
>
> "I am _____" (e.g., *giving, taking, being,* etc.)
>
> **Past Participle:** the past tense form of a verb that will fit into the sentence
>
> "I have _____" (e.g., *walked, given, taken, been,* etc.)

### Participial Phrase

A participial phrase is a group of words beginning with a participle that works together to act as an adjective. The participle in a participial phrase acts like both a verb (it can take a direct object or indirect object, or be modified by an adverb, but it will never have a subject) **and** an adjective (it modifies a noun).

Participles and participial phrases, like all adjectives, can be removed from the sentence, and it will still be grammatically correct.

**Example 1:**  The whistle *shrieking at top volume* tells the fireman there is an emergency.

The whistle tells the fireman there is an emergency.

*Shrieking at top volume* is not grammatically necessary—the sentence still makes perfect sense without it—but it adds information to the sentence that helps to create a mood. We know that this is not a quiet, peaceful little whistle. It's loud and urgent, and it means emergency!

**Diagramming Participles and Participial Phrases**

If you find a participle all by itself in a sentence, you would call it an adjective because that's how it acts (e.g., ***walking*** shoes, ***given*** name). Diagram it just like you would any other adjective:

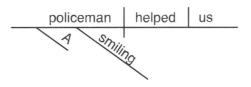

Example 2:

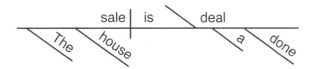

Example 3:

If the participle is part of a participial phrase, it is diagrammed in a different way. First, identify and underline the entire participial phrase. A participial phrase acts as an adjective, so it will be attached first to what it is modifying. Bend the participle in the middle on a "dogleg" as shown here:

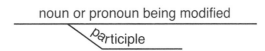

After that, diagram the other parts of the participial phrase as you have learned. Here are examples of how to diagram different participial phrases:

**Example 4:** **Participle with direct object**

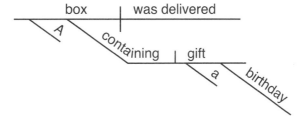

*Notice that the participle is still parsed with *v* as you learned in Level 3, and not with *av*. It's still a verbal even though now you know what kind of verbal it is and what it's doing. It has a direct object (*gift*) but no subject. You might think *box* is the subject of *containing*, but if we just take the part of the sentence with the subject of the sentence and add the participial phrase, we have "A box containing a birthday gift." That isn't a complete sentence. Say it out loud and you will be left thinking, "What **about** the box containing the birthday gift?" The present participle, *containing*, is the wrong form of the verb to be acting as a verb by itself. It needs a helping verb to act as a verb. By itself, it tells us more about the box that was delivered, so it is acting as an adjective. But it's also acting like a verb. It has a direct object that answers the question "*containing **what**?*" That's the very definition of a participle: a verb form acting like both a verb and an adjective.

**Example 5:** **Participle with its own modifiers**

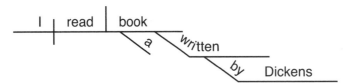

> *pro av art n v pp pn*
> I read a book written (by <u>Dickens</u>).

In this example, the participial phrase includes the participle and a prepositional phrase modifying it. Just like verbs, a participle can be modified by an adverb (or a prepositional phrase acting like one).

**Example 6:** **Participial phrase with predicate nominative or predicate adjective**

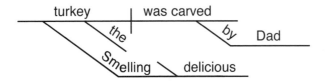

> *v adj art n hv av pp pn*
> <u>Smelling</u> <u>delicious</u>, the turkey was carved (by Dad).

Look at the participial phrase "*Smelling delicious.*" Participles are **always** adjectives and they **always** act like the verbs they are, in every way, **except** for having a subject. Although *smelling* is not acting as the main verb of this sentence, it still belongs to the group of verbs that are always linking verbs, so it can take a predicate adjective. *Smelling delicious* tells us more about the turkey.

**Note:** When a participial phrase is **introductory** (it comes at the beginning of the sentence), it is set off from the rest of the sentence by a comma.

On the next page, you'll find a chart to help you keep track of the three different verbals you are learning. For this lesson, use your notes to complete the information about participial phrases.

# The Verbals

| Type of Verbal | What Does It Look Like? | What Job Does It Do? | How Is It Diagramed? | Can It Be Removed? |
|---|---|---|---|---|
| **Participle** (Lesson 1) | *Verb + -ing* or *Fits into "I have _____"* | *Modifier (modifies nouns or pronouns)* | | *Removeable* |
| **Gerund** (Lesson 2) | *Verb + -ing* | *Noun* | | *Not Removeable* |
| **Infinitive** (Lesson 3) | *to + verb* | *Modifier* | | *Removeable* |
| | | *Noun* | | *Not Removeable* |

*Your student should complete the information in this chart after each lesson. If they need help, give them hints or show them how to complete it correctly.*

# Participial Phrases: Exercise A

**Directions**

Look at each verb below. If it is a present participle, mark **pres** in the space at the left. If it is a past participle, mark **past** in the space. If the verb is neither kind of participle, mark **verb**. Look back at the definitions in the notes for help.

1) _____ spinning
    *pres*

2) _____ heard
    *past*

3) _____ having
    *pres*

4) _____ behave
    *verb*

5) _____ look
    *verb*

6) _____ was
    *verb*

7) _____ has gone
    *verb*

8) _____ win
    *verb*

9) _____ placed
    *past*

10) _____ could
    *verb*

**Directions**

Parse the sentences below and put prepositional phrases in parentheses. Underline participial phrases. Write what noun or pronoun each participial phrase is modifying. Then diagram each sentence.

*Diagramming solutions are found at the end of this book.*

        *v     art    n    art  n    adv    av*

**11)** Outrunning the hounds, the fox easily escaped.
    *fox*

    *pro av pro    v     adv     pp art   n*

**12)** I saw him fishing contentedly (by the river).
    *him*
    **Note:** *If your student doesn't underline by the river as part of the participial phrase, count it correct as long as they identify fishing contentedly. A successful argument could be made that it is modifying saw rather than fishing.*

    *v    pp art  adj    n   art     n     av   art   n*

**13)** Tackled (on the one-yard line), the quarterback fumbled the ball.
    *quarterback*

14)
   *adv*      *v*    *pp*  *art*   *n*   *pro*   *av*   *adj*    *n*

**14)** Wildly cheering (for the team), we celebrated their victory.
    *we*

   *art*   *n*   *av*   *art*   *n*   *art* *n*    *v*    *pp* *adj*    *n*   *conj*  *v*   *pp*  *adj*    *n*

**15)** The clerk handed the customer a box wrapped (in white paper) and tied (with red ribbon).
    *box (This is an example of a compound participial phrase.)*

This sentence is an excellent one for demonstrating what a **dangling participle** is. If we move the participial phrases, as in, *Wrapped in white paper and tied with a red ribbon, the clerk handed the customer a box,* we get a pretty funny mental picture here of a clerk decoratively wrapped like a gift! That's because the participial phrases are "dangling" out there next to the wrong noun. Like any other adjective, participial phrases must be next to the noun or pronoun they modify; otherwise, they appear to modify the noun they are near.

   *v*   *art*  *n*   *pp* *adj*   *n*   *art*  *n*   *av*   *adv*   *pp*   *art*    *n*

**16)** Balancing a book (on her head), the girl walked slowly (across the room).
    *girl*

   *art*    *n*    *av*  *art* *n*    *v*    *adj*    *n*  *pp* *art*  *n*

**17)** The professor wrote a note expressing her approval (of the plan).
    *note*

   *art*    *n*    *av*  *art*   *n*     *v*   *pp* *art*    *n*

**18)** The children found an arrowhead buried (on the riverbank).
    *arrowhead*

**Directions**

Write what job the following words are doing in the sentences in the previous section. Choose your answers from among the following:

| subject | object of the preposition | verb |
| modifier | direct object | indirect object |
| predicate nominative | predicate adjective | |

| Sentence # | Word | Job |
|---|---|---|
| 11 | fox | *subject* |
| 12 | contentedly | *modifier* |
| 13 | line | *object of the preposition* |
| 14 | Wildly | *modifier* |
| 14 | cheering | *modifier* |
| 15 | customer | *indirect object* |
| 15 | box | *direct object* |
| 16 | girl | *subject* |
| 17 | wrote | *verb* |
| 18 | arrowhead | *direct object* |

**Directions**

*Answers will vary; an example is provided.*

19) Make up a participial phrase to modify the **subject** of the following sentence. Diagram the subject and participial phrase. Look at your notes if you need help.

The coach, _____, signalled a timeout.
   *gesturing wildly*

20) Make up a participial phrase to modify the **direct object** of the following sentence. Diagram the direct object and participial phrase. Look at your notes if you need help.

I have three friends _____.
   *taking the honors class*

# Participial Phrases: Exercise B

## Directions

Parse the sentences below and put the prepositional phrases in parentheses. Underline the participial phrases. Diagram the sentences. Use your Process Chart and the lesson notes to help you.

*Diagramming solutions are found at the end of this book.*

        *v      adv    pp  art     n     art     n     av    art    n*

**1)** <u>Smiling happily</u> (at the audience), the actress accepted the flowers.

        *hv   pro   av   pn    v   adj    n     adv*

**2)** Did you see Fred <u>riding his bicycle</u> today?

*Today could modify either did see or riding; either can be counted as correct. If it is modifying riding, it should be underlined.*

    *art     n    v    pp art  adj    n   conj    adv       v      lv  art  n  pp  art     n*

**3)** The cake, <u>baked</u> (by a master chef) and <u>beautifully decorated</u>, was the hit (of the party).

     *v   art  adj     n   pro  adv    av   adj    n    pp    adj     n*

**4)** <u>Being a devout pacifist</u>, I naturally avoid any contact (with violent people).

As we have already mentioned, participles still have the characteristics of the verbs they are. *Being* is therefore a "linking verbal," and *pacifist* is a predicate nominative because *pacifist* and *I* are the same person.

     *adv     av   adj     n     v    pp   adj      n     pp   adj   n*

**5)** Please read three books <u>written</u> (by American authors) (during this year).

This sentence has a good example of **ambiguity.** Ambiguity means that something can be interpreted more than one way. Does this sentence mean that the books must have been **written** this year, or does it simply mean to complete the **reading** during this year, regardless of when the books were written? What if you were taking a college class and your entire grade depended on following these instructions—would you be confident that you have the right interpretation? Can you think of any way to word this so there's no more confusion?

       *v    pp  art   n   pp  adj    n     pn   av  art     n     pp  adj   n*

**6)** <u>Screeching</u> (at the top) (of her lungs), Tillie hit the mugger (with her bag).

      *av   art    n     v    pp   adj     n    adj    n   pp     n*

**7)** Give the lady <u>seated</u> (by my mother) this glass (of lemonade).

v   art adj   n   pp    n    pp  art  n   pn    av    adv  conj    av

**8)** Choosing a huge piece (of chocolate) (from the box), Mimi yawned lazily and continued

*adj    n*

her reading.

**Directions**

Write what job the following words are doing in the previous sentences. Choose your answers from among the following:

*subject*      *object of the preposition*      *verb*

*modifier*      *direct object*      *indirect object*

*predicate nominative*      *predicate adjective*

| Sentence # | Word | Job |
|---|---|---|
| 1 | flowers | *direct object* |
| 2 | bicycle | *direct object* |
| 3 | hit | *predictate nominative* |
| 4 | pacifist | *predictate nominative* |
| 4 | contact | *direct object* |
| 5 | books | *direct object* |
| 6 | lungs | *object of the preposition* |
| 7 | lady | *indirect object* |
| 7 | glass | *direct object* |
| 8 | lazily | *modifier* |

**Short Answer**

*Answers will vary; one example is given.*

**9)** Make up a participial phrase to modify the indirect object of the following sentence.

I told the students _____
a story.

    *seated in front of me*

# Participial Phrases: Exercise C

**Directions**

Parse the sentences below and put prepositional phrases in parentheses. Underline the participial phrases. Diagram the sentences. Use your Process Chart and the lesson notes if you need help.

*Diagramming solutions are found at the end of this book.*

     *v*    *art* *adj*    *n*    *art*    *n*      *av*    *pp*   *art*   *n*

**1)** <u>Carrying a large package</u>, the messenger stumbled (across the room).

    *art*    *n*     *v*    *pp* *art*    *n*   *pp*  *n*    *av*   *adv* *pp* *art*    *n*

**2)** The dog, <u>attracted (by the smell) (of meat)</u>, trotted over (to the stranger).

    *art*   *n*     *v*    *n*  *pp* *art*  *adj*    *n*    *av*   *pro*

**3)** The men <u>playing golf (at the country club)</u> helped us.

    *pro*   *av*   *art* *adj*    *n*      *v*    *adv*  *pp* *art*  *n*

**4)** We noticed an old cowboy <u>tanned deeply (by the sun)</u>.

    *art*   *n*  *hv*    *av*    *pp*    *n*     *adv*     *v*   *conj*   *v*   *pp*     *n*

**5)** The store was packed (with customers) <u>Christmas shopping</u> and <u>looking (for bargains)</u>.

    *v*    *adv*    *adj* *pp* *adj*   *n*    *art*    *n*    *av*  *art*   *n*

**6)** <u>Feeling suddenly bored (by her guests)</u>, the hostess stifled a yawn.

    *pro*  *pp* *adj*   *n*    *v*    *n*  *lv* *adj*    *n*

**7)** Which (of those men) <u>wearing suits</u> is your boss?

    *v*   *pro* *art*    *n*      *v*    *pp* *adj*    *n*  *conj*   *adj*      *n*

**8)** Bring me a sundae <u>smothered (in hot fudge and whipped cream)</u>.

    *hv* *art*  *n*     *v*    *art*  *n*   *adv* *av*  *pp*  *adj*    *n*

**9)** Did a lady <u>carrying a baby</u> just run (by this house)?

adv   v   pp   adj   n   pn   av   pp   adj   n   adj   n

**10)** Easily tired (since her operation), Emily rested (in her room) (after lunch).

**Directions**

Write what job each word is doing in the previous sentences. Choose your answers from among the following:

| subject | object of the preposition | verb |
|---|---|---|
| modifier | direct object | indirect object |
| predicate nominative | predicate adjective | |

| Sentence # | Word | Job |
|---|---|---|
| 1 | package | *direct object* |
| 2 | meat | *object of the preposition* |
| 2 | stranger | *object of the preposition* |
| 3 | men | *subject* |
| 3 | us | *direct object* |
| 4 | deeply | *modifier* |
| 5 | was packed | *verb* |
| 6 | bored | *predicate adjective* |
| 7 | suits | *direct object* |
| 8 | hot | *modifier* |
| 9 | house | *object of the preposition* |
| 10 | Emily | *subject* |

**Short Answer**

**11)** Make up a participial phrase to modify the **predicate nominative** in the following sentence:
*Answers will vary; one example is given.*

He was an old man _____.
*sitting peacefully in the sunshine*

**12)** Make up a participial phrase to modify the **object of the preposition** in the following sentence:
*Answers will vary; one example is given.*

I sent a letter to my aunt _____.
*living in Germany*

# Application & Enrichment

## Verb Tenses: Simple Present and Simple Past Tense

Verbs are action words—but not all action happens live, at this moment in time. Some things happened in the past, while other things will happen in the future. Some things started happening in the past and will continue happening into the future. The verb forms we use to indicate **when** an action happened are called **verb tenses**. When we see or hear them, we know if an action started and finished in the past, if it hasn't started happening yet, or if it's happening right now.

Over the next few Application & Enrichment lessons, we'll update this chart for you as we talk about different verb tenses. It will show you the focus of that day's lessons and remind you of what you have already learned.

| *to walk* | **present** | **past** | **future** |
|---|---|---|---|
| **simple** | walk | walked | |
| **perfect** | | | |
| **progressive** | | | |
| **perfect progressive** | | | |

The least complicated verb tense is called the **simple tense**: it's "simply" the verb, with no helping verbs. The first two tenses we will look at are the **simple present** and **simple past.**

For these two tenses, **regular verbs** are **conjugated** (*to give all the different forms of a particular verb and tense*) like this:

| subject | present tense<br>*(no change except 3rd person singular)* | past tense<br>*(add -**ed** for all)* |
|---|---|---|
| I | walk | walked |
| you | walk | walked |
| he/she/it | walks (*add –(e)s*) | walked |
| we | walk | walked |
| they | walk | walked |

Simple, right? In present tense, the form only changes for the third person singular, meaning *he/she/it*. In the past tense, it adds *-ed* for all subjects.

English does have quite a few **irregular verbs**, or verbs that don't follow the easy pattern shown above. The irregularity is almost always shown in the past tense form of the verb. Rather than adding -ed to create the past tense, the verb changes its spelling. There are three verbs that are irregular in the third-person singular. Examples of irregular verbs and the way they change are shown in the following table:

| Examples: | simple present tense | | simple past tense | |
|---|---|---|---|---|
| **to have** | he has | we have | he had | we had |
| **to do** | he does | we do | he did | we did |
| **to go** | he goes | we go | he went | we went |
| **to write** | he writes | we write | he wrote | we wrote |
| **to swim** | he swims | we swim | he swam | we swam |
| **to see** | he sees | we see | he saw | we saw |

If there is more than one verb in a sentence, be sure that they agree in tense. For example:

Incorrect: The dog **was** so excited to play fetch that he **runs** around in circles of joy.

(The verbs don't agree in tense: **was** is past tense; **runs** is present tense.)

Correct: The dog **was** so excited to play fetch that he **ran** around in circles of joy. (Both **was** and **ran** are past tense.)

or: The dog **is** so excited to play fetch that he **runs** around in circles of joy. (Both **is** and **runs** are present tense.)

**Directions**

Circle the verb(s) in each sentence. Write whether the sentence is present tense or past tense.

**1)** I (want) a hippopotamus for Christmas.

*present*

**2)** My best present ever (was) my pink bicycle with the banana seat.

*past*

**3)** He (drove) recklessly along the clifftop road and narrowly (avoided) disaster.

*past*

**4)** I (have) a craving for Mom's Yorkshire puddings.

*present*

**5)** Janelle (enjoys) shopping, dining out, and visiting new places on her vacation.

*present*

**Directions**

Change each of the verbs in the sentences above to the other tense. For example, if the sentence above is present tense, write the past tense form of the verb(s) below. If the sentence is past tense, write the present tense form(s).

**6)** _____*wanted*_____

**7)** _____*is*_____

**8)** _____*drives, avoids*_____

**9)** _____*had*_____

**10)** _____*enjoyed*_____

# Participial Phrases: Assessment

## Directions

Parse the sentences below and put parentheses around the prepositional phrases. Underline the participial phrases. Diagram the sentences. Remember to use your Process Chart and lesson notes if you need help. *Each correctly identified word, prepositional phrase, or participial phrase is worth one point.*

*Diagramming solutions are found at the end of this book.*

          adv       av    pro  pp adj    n      v    art adj     n

**1)** Please introduce me (to that man) <u>wearing the blue sweater</u>.

___
12

      art    n    lv       adj     n      v    art     n      adj   n   pp art    n

**2)** The thief was either that man <u>carrying the briefcase</u> or that boy (with the bike).

___
16
                           conj

        v     pp   n   art    n   lv  adv    adj

**3)** <u>Painted</u> (in oils), the picture was very beautiful.

___
10

        adv    pro   av      n     v   pp  art  adj   adj       n

**4)** Yesterday we heard speeches <u>given</u> (by the major political candidates).

___
12

      pro av adj   n     v   pp    pn   art   adj        n

**5)** I sent my cousin <u>living</u> (in Germany) a graduation announcement.

___
12

        v    art   n   conj    v   art  n  adv art adj   n     av     pp    n

**6)** <u>Winding the clock</u> and <u>putting the cat out</u>, the old man prepared (for bed).

___
17

      pro  lv art     n      v   pp    n

**7)** It was a marriage <u>made</u> (in heaven).

___
9

        v       adj   pp art    n    art   n    av      pp     pro    pp art  n

**8)** <u>Becoming conscious</u> (of the smoke), the boy looked (around himself) (for a fire).

___
17

      lv art     n      v    adj  adj    n    adj   n

**9)** Is the woman <u>wearing that fur coat</u> your aunt?

___
10

      art   n     v      pp art adj   n     av    adv   pp   art    n

**10)** The boy, <u>munching</u> (on a large roll), ambled slowly (down the street).

___
15

═══
130

## Directions

Write what job each word is doing in the previous sentences. Choose your answers from among the following:

| | | |
|---|---|---|
| *subject* | *object of the preposition* | *verb* |
| *modifier* | *direct object* | *indirect object* |
| *predicate nominative* | *predicate adjective* | |

*Five points each*

| Sentence # | Word | Job |
|:---:|:---:|:---:|
| 1 | introduce | *verb* |
| 1 | sweater | *direct object* |
| 2 | man | *predicate nominative* |
| 3 | beautiful | *predicate adjective* |
| 4 | we | *subject* |
| 4 | speeches | *direct object* |
| 5 | cousin | *indirect object* |
| 5 | announcement | *direct object* |
| 6 | clock | *direct object* |
| 7 | It | *subject* |
| 7 | marriage | *predicate nominative* |
| 8 | conscious | *predicate adjective* |
| 9 | fur | *modifier* |
| 9 | aunt | *predicate nominative* |
| 10 | boy | *subject* |
| 10 | roll | *object of the preposition* |

═══

*80*

## Diagrams

*Enter score from diagramming solutions here.*

═══

*98*

═══ *Total Points*  $\dfrac{246}{308} = 80\%$
*308*

## Lesson 2
# Gerund Phrases

### Instructor Notes

Students may have a hard time keeping the three verbals straight in their minds. Gerunds end with -*ing*, just like present participles, so it's understandable to be confused. When students apply what they know about the jobs words and phrases do in sentences, it will become clearer for them. Be sure that they complete the gerund row in their verbals chart. Identifying the distinguishing features of gerund phrases will help lessen any confusion.

*Diagramming solutions are found after Lesson 7.*

### A Tip for Instructors

If a lesson seems overwhelming, slow the pace a bit and have your student split up each exercise by doing the odd-numbered sentences one day and even-numbered the next. This will give your student two weeks to complete the lesson instead of one.

# Lesson 2: Gerund Phrases

Another kind of verbal is the **gerund**, a verb form ending in *-ing*.

But wait—isn't a present participle a verb form ending in *-ing*? You are correct— great work! But a **gerund** is used as a noun, not as an adjective. Also, unlike the participle, it can't be removed without changing the grammatical structure of the sentence, possibly even making it grammatically incorrect.

**Gerunds**
A gerund is a verb ending in *-ing* which is used as a noun. It cannot be removed from the sentence without changing its grammatical structure. Gerunds can do all the jobs that nouns or pronouns can do: direct object, indirect object, object of the preposition, or predicate nominative. If a sentence has a gerund by itself, diagram it as you would any noun.

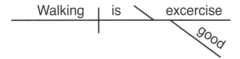

**Example A:**

*v  lv  adj  n*

Walking is good exercise.

*Walking*, which is usually thought of as a verb, is the subject of the above N-LV-N sentence.

Here's an example of *walking* as the predicate nominative:

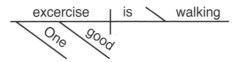

**Example B:**

*adj  adj  n  lv  v*

One good exercise is walking.

Like all verbals, gerunds also act like verbs in many ways. For example, they can take a direct object or be modified by adverbs. When they behave like verbs *and* nouns, the gerund and all of its modifiers and objects are called a **gerund phrase**.

**Gerund phrases**
A gerund phrase includes a gerund and all of its modifiers and objects. The complete phrase works together as one unit to do one of the jobs of a noun (subject, direct object, indirect object, object of the preposition, or predicate nominative).

Gerund phrases are diagrammed in a special way. The gerund phrase is doing the job of a noun, so put it up on a stilt above the place for the noun. The gerund itself is broken into two steps, with the verb part on the higher step and the *-ing* on the same line as the rest of the phrase. That may sound confusing, so here's what it looks like for each of the jobs that nouns do.

**Example 1:**     **Gerund phrase as subject**

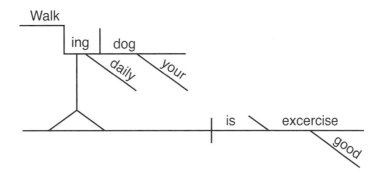

    *v*    *adj*   *n*   *adv*  *lv*  *adj*    *n*

Walking your dog daily is good exercise.

The entire gerund phrase *Walking your dog daily* is the subject, so it all needs to go in the subject space. Use the stilt to make that possible and still show the complete phrase as one unit. (Remember, a phrase is a group of words that act as one unit!) *Walking* is broken into two steps, with *Walk* on the higher one and *-ing* on the same line as the rest of the phrase.

**Example 2:**     **Gerund phrase as direct object**

   *pn*    *av*    *v*    *art*   *n*

John loves walking the dog.

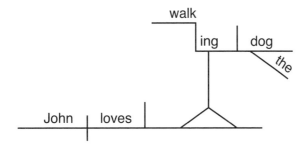

The entire gerund phrase *walking the dog* is the direct object.

**Example 3:**     **Gerund phrase as predicate nominative**

   *adj*   *adj*    *n*   *lv*   *v*   *art*   *n*

John's favorite chore is walking the dog.

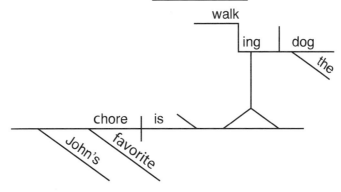

**Example 4:**     Gerund phrase as object of the preposition

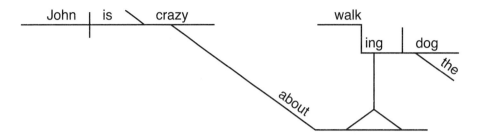

    *pn*  *lv*  *adj*   *pp*     *v*   *art*   *n*

John is crazy (about walking the dog).

**Example 5:**     Gerund phrase as indirect object

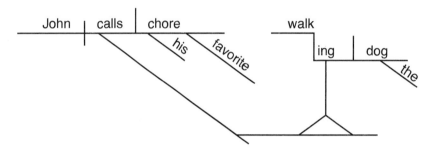

    *pn*   *av*    *v*    *art*  *n*  *adj*  *adj*    *n*

John calls walking the dog his favorite chore.

Boy, that John sure is crazy about walking his dog! So remember, when you have just a gerund, diagram it just like you would a noun. When you have a complete gerund phrase, however, you need to use the stilt with the steps so you can diagram the entire phrase but still show it together as one unit.

Now complete the **Gerund** row on your Verbal Phrases chart.

# Gerund Phrases: Exercise A

## Directions

Parse the sentences below and put prepositional phrases in parentheses. Underline the gerund phrases. Write what job the gerund phrase is doing in each sentence.

      *v        n    lv art adj   n   pp adj     n*

**1)** Writing essays is a major part (of our course).

    *subject*

      *v    art   n    pp   n    hv    av     pro*

**2)** Playing the radio (at night) may disturb others.

    *subject*

    *pro hv  adv    av     v      n*

**3)** I have always enjoyed playing chess.

    *direct object*

    *art   n   av adv pp   v    art   n  art n*

**4)** The thief got in (by telling the guard a lie).

    *object of the preposition*

    *adj   n   hv  adv   lv    v    n     adv    pp adj    n*

**5)** His hobby has always been arguing politics heatedly (with his friends).

    *predicate nominative*

    *art   n   av  pro   n    pp    v     pn*

**6)** The class gave me practice (in speaking Spanish).

    *object of the preposition*

    *pn     av    v    n  art adj   n*

**7)** Mortimer gives playing guitar a bad name.

    *indirect object*

**Directions**

Parse the sentences below and put the prepositional phrases in parentheses. Underline the gerund phrases. Diagram the sentences. Use your notes and The Process Chart if you need help.

    *adj     v    art   n   pp  art    n      av    art    n*

**8)** Molly's <u>rattling the dishes</u> (in the kitchen) awakened the baby.

    *adj   adj     n    lv   v    pro   adj    n*

**9)** Her favorite pastime is <u>telling everyone her troubles</u>.

    *pro  av     v    art  adj    n*

**10)** I dislike <u>teasing the little boy</u>.

# Gerund Phrases: Exercise B

## Directions

In this exercise, each sentence has both a gerund phrase and a participial phrase. You will need to identify which is which. To do that, determine whether the verbal phrase is doing the job of a noun (gerund) or is modifying a noun (participial). If you're not sure, remember that a good test is to see if it can be removed from the sentence without leaving the sentence grammatically incorrect. If you can remove it, it's a participial phrase.

Parse the sentences below and put the prepositional phrases in parentheses. Underline the participial phrases **once** and the gerund phrases **twice**. Diagram the sentences. Use your Process Chart and lesson notes if you need help.

      *v   art   n    pp  art adj   n    pn   av    v      n*

1) Being a man (with a big heart), Jim likes helping people.

      *v     art  adj    n     v   pp art   n   lv  art    adj    n  pp     n*

2) Rescuing the stray dog begging (in the street) was the woman's act (of kindness)

  *pp   art   n*

(for the day).

     *adj     n      adv     v    pp     n      av  art    n    pp   v   adj     n*

3) My counselor, carefully trained (in psychology), knows the importance (of sharing your troubles).

      *v   art    adj      n   pro  av   v    pp art     n*

4) Being an incurable romantic, I love walking (in the moonlight).

      *v   pp  art   n     adv      av      n    v   pp art   n*

5) Crying (in the movies) usually embarasses people caught (in the act).

   *art  adj   n  pp adj   n    v    pp art   n    lv    v    art    n   pp  art    n*

6) The last act (of their day) spent (in the desert) was watching the sunset (from the mesa).

**Directions**

Write what job the following words are doing in each sentence. Choose your answers from among the following:

| subject | object of the preposition | verb |
|---|---|---|
| modifier | direct object | indirect object |
| predicate nominative | predicate adjective | |

| Sentence # | Word | Job |
|---|---|---|
| 1 | man | *predicate nominative* |
| 1 | people | *direct object* |
| 2 | street | *object of the preposition* |
| 2 | woman's | *modifier* |
| 2 | kindness | *object of the preposition* |
| 3 | importance | *direct object* |
| 4 | incurable | *modifier* |
| 4 | romantic | *predicate nominative* |
| 5 | usually | *modifier* |
| 5 | act | *object of the preposition* |
| 6 | desert | *object of the preposition* |

# Gerund Phrases: Exercise C

## Directions

Parse the sentences below and put parentheses around the prepositional phrases. Underline the participial phrases **once** and the gerund phrases **twice**. Diagram the sentences.

       *n     v     adv     pp  art    n     hv    av   pp    v    art     n*

**1)**  Flowers picked especially (for the occasion) were used (for decorating the ballroom).

       *adj    n     v    pp   adj    n   lv     v       n    pp    n*

**2)**  My hobby, developed (over many years), is embroidering samplers (on linen).

      ——*pn*——    *av     v     n     v    pp  art  adj     n*

**3)**  Mr. Gardner enjoys reading books written (in the 18th century).

       *adv     v   art  adj     n     av   pro     v    pp art    adj*

**4)**  Fluently speaking a foreign language gives anyone (interested (in a diplomatic

   *n   art  adj     n*

career) a distinct advantage.

      *adj     n     v     n    pp art   pn    av    v   art  adj     n*

**5)**  Many students attending college (in the Fifties) made stuffing a telephone booth

   *art adj   n*

a huge fad.

      *pro  av    ——pn——    pp    v   adj  adj   n     v   adv pp art     n*

**6)**  I helped Mrs. Willows (by visiting her little boy) cooped up (in the hospital).

**Directions**

Write what job the following words are doing in each sentence. Choose your answers from among the following:

| | | |
|---|---|---|
| subject | object of the preposition | verb |
| modifier | direct object | indirect object |
| predicate nominative | predicate adjective | |

| Sentence # | Word | Job |
|:---:|:---:|:---:|
| 1 | occasion | object of the preposition |
| 1 | ballroom | direct object |
| 2 | hobby | subject |
| 2 | many | modifier |
| 3 | books | direct object |
| 4 | language | direct object |
| 4 | advantage | direct object |
| 5 | made | verb |
| 5 | fad | direct object |
| 6 | boy | direct object |
| 6 | hospital | object of the preposition |

# Application & Enrichment

## Verb Tenses: Present Perfect and Past Perfect

The next verb tense to look at is the **perfect tense**. That doesn't mean that this tense is better than all of the other tenses! In this case, *perfect* comes from the Latin word *perfectum,* which means *completed.* We use the perfect tense to show actions that have been started, and sometimes completed, in the past.

The **present perfect tense** is formed by using the **present tense** of the helping verb *to have* plus the past participle of the verb (usually formed by adding *-ed*). It describes two possible scenarios:

1)  an action that started in the past and continues up to the present time
    **Example:**  I have skied for years. (I started skiing in the past, and I still ski today.)

2)  an action that was completed in the past at a nonspecific time
    **Example:**  I have read all of the books in that series. (I read the books in the past, and I finished reading them before today.)

The **past perfect tense** is formed by using the **past tense** of the helping verb *to have* plus the past participle of the verb. It describes an action that was completed in the past that occurs *before* something else that happened in the past. The context needs to make clear that there is a sequence of events.

> **Examples:**  The princess looked for the frog, but it had jumped back into the pond. (The frog jumped back into the pond **before** the princess looked for it.)
>
> The teacher said that Friday was the last day to hand in book reports. I had already handed mine in. (I handed it in **before** the teacher said that Friday was the last day.)

Notice that the events don't have to be in the same sentence!

The helping verb *have* determines whether or not the verb is present tense or past tense. The main verb is in past participle form.

| to walk | present | past | future |
|---|---|---|---|
| **simple** | walk | walked | |
| **perfect** | have walked<br>*have/has* + past participle | had walked<br>*had* + past participle | |
| **progressive** | | | |
| **perfect progressive** | | | |

This tense used to be called the **pluperfect** and is still called that in other languages. You may come across this word if you study other languages or read old grammar books (which we all do, just for fun, right?).

**Directions**

The following sentences are written in present tense. Rewrite them using the present perfect tense for the verbs in italics.

**1)** I *walk* to school every day.

*I have walked to school every day.*

**2)** The road crew *repairs* the potholes on my street.

*The road crew has repaired the potholes on my street.*

**3)** The screen on my phone *cracks* because I keep dropping it.

*The screen on my phone has cracked because I keep dropping it.*

**4)** We *travel* to watch the big game against our arch rival in person.

*We have traveled to watch the big game against our arch rival in person.*

**5)** Josh and Mary *see* the sign announcing the grand opening of the new bakery.

*Josh and Mary have seen the sign announcing the grand opening of the new bakery.*

**Directions**

The following sentences are written in past tense. Rewrite them using the past perfect tense for the verbs in italics.

**6)** I *spent* all of the money I had on a miniature donkey.

*I had spent all of the money I had on a miniature donkey.*

**7)** The cat *climbed* even higher in the tree by the time the firemen arrived.

*The cat had climbed even higher in the tree by the time the firemen arrived.*

**8)** Before my alarm went off, I *awoke* with a start.

*Before my alarm went off, I had awoken with a start.*

**9)** The plaster *set* by the time we were ready to use it.

*The plaster had set by the time we were ready to use it.*

**10)** We *received* a birthday card from Aunt Shirley every year until we turned eighteen.

*We had received a birthday card from Aunt Shirley every year until we turned eighteen.*

# Gerund Phrases: Assessment

## Directions

Parse the sentences below and put parentheses around the prepositional phrases. Underline the participial phrases once and the gerund phrases twice. Diagram the sentences. Use The Process Chart and your lesson notes if you need help.

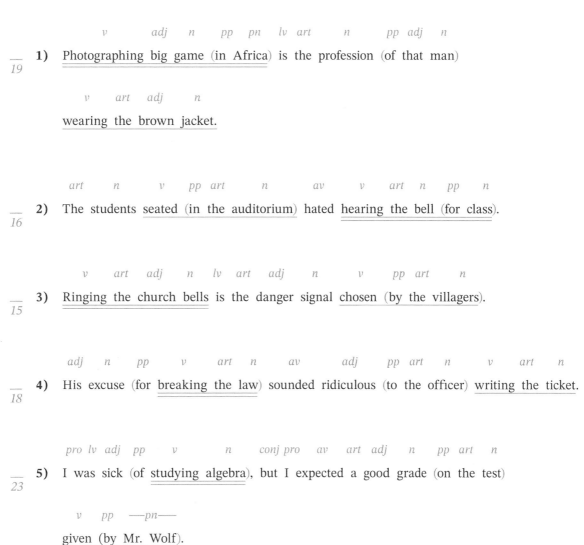

            *v*      *adj*    *n*    *pp*  *pn*   *lv*  *art*     *n*     *pp*  *adj*    *n*

**1)** Photographing big game (in Africa) is the profession (of that man)
___
19

           *v*     *art*   *adj*     *n*

wearing the brown jacket.

         *art*     *n*     *v*   *pp*  *art*     *n*       *av*     *v*    *art*   *n*   *pp*     *n*

**2)** The students seated (in the auditorium) hated hearing the bell (for class).
___
16

           *v*    *art*   *adj*     *n*    *lv*  *art*   *adj*     *n*      *v*    *pp*  *art*     *n*

**3)** Ringing the church bells is the danger signal chosen (by the villagers).
___
15

         *adj*    *n*    *pp*      *v*    *art*   *n*     *av*      *adj*    *pp*  *art*   *n*     *v*   *art*     *n*

**4)** His excuse (for breaking the law) sounded ridiculous (to the officer) writing the ticket.
___
18

         *pro*  *lv*  *adj*  *pp*      *v*        *n*    *conj*  *pro*   *av*   *art*  *adj*     *n*    *pp*  *art*   *n*

**5)** I was sick (of studying algebra), but I expected a good grade (on the test)
___
23

           *v*    *pp*    ──*pn*──

given (by Mr. Wolf).

           *v*     *n*     *pp*    *n*    *lv*  *art*   *adj*     *n*     *pp*  *adj*    *n*    *v*    *pp*    *adj*       *n*

**6)** Playing tricks (on people) is the major pastime (of my cousin) going (to boarding school).
___
20

         *art*    *n*     *v*     *pp*   *art*   *adj*     *n*    *adv*    *av*     *v*   *art*    *n*

**7)** The car speeding (down a narrow road) just missed hitting a child.
___
15

        *pn*   *av*   *adj*   *n*   *v*   *art*  *adj*  *n*  *pp*   *v*   *adj*   *n*

__  **8)**  Jan helped her friend catching the early plane (by ironing her dress).
15

        *adj*   *n*   *adv*   *v*  *pp*  *art*  *n*   *av*   *v*   *art* *adj*  *n*  *pp* *pro*

__  **9)**  My horse, recently broken (to the saddle), enjoys exploring the bridle paths (with me).
18

        *pn*   *v*   *pp* *adj*  *n*   *pp*  *n*   *av*   *v*   *n*

__  **10)**  Mother, accustomed (to large groups) (of people), adores planning parties.
14

══
173

**Directions**

Write what jobs the following words are doing in each sentence. Choose your answers from among the following:

<table>
<tr><td>*subject*</td><td>*object of the preposition*</td><td>*verb*</td></tr>
<tr><td>*modifier*</td><td>*direct object*</td><td>*indirect object*</td></tr>
<tr><td>*predicate nominative*</td><td>*predicate adjective*</td><td></td></tr>
</table>

*Five points each*

| Sentence # | Word | Job |
|:---:|:---:|:---:|
| 1 | game | *direct object* |
| 1 | Africa | *object of the preposition* |
| 1 | profession | *predicate nominative* |
| 3 | signal | *predicate nominative* |
| 4 | excuse | *subject* |
| 4 | law | *direct object* |
| 4 | ridiculous | *predicate adjective* |
| 5 | sick | *predicate adjective* |
| 5 | expected | *verb* |
| 5 | grade | *direct object* |
| 6 | people | *object of the preposition* |
| 6 | boarding | *modifier* |
| 7 | child | *direct object* |
| 8 | Jan | *subject* |
| 9 | horse | *subject* |
| 10 | people | *object of the preposition* |

*80*

### Diagrams

*Enter score from diagramming solutions here.*

$$\overline{\overline{\phantom{xxx}}}$$
*131*

$$\underline{\phantom{xxx}} \textit{Total Points} \quad \frac{306}{384} = 80\%$$
*384*

## Lesson 3
# Infinitive Phrases

### Instructor Notes

The only thing tricky about infinitives is that they are two words: *to* and a verb. Students are familiar with *to* as a preposition, but when followed by a verb, it is an essential part of an infinitive. Unlike participial and gerund phrases, infinitive phrases can do more than one job. They can be either a modifier or a noun, doing any of the jobs those words can do. If an infinitive phrase can be removed from the sentence without changing the meaning, it is a modifier. If it can't be removed from the sentence, it is acting as a noun.

*Diagramming solutions are found after Lesson 7.*

---

**A Tip for Instructors**

Consider asking your student to diagram half of the sentences in an exercise; if they understand the concept and can identify the word, phrase, or clause that is the focus of the lesson, they may not need to diagram every sentence.

## Lesson 3: Infinitive Phrases

The final verbal we need to know is the **infinitive**. It usually has two words: the word *to,* followed by the root form of the verb. The "root form" means the verb without any tenses or number agreement, just the simple verb you would find in the dictionary entry. Sometimes the word *to* is left out, but if it is there, it is always part of the infinitive.

> **Infinitive**
> The infinitive is a verb form, almost always preceded by *to*, that is used as a noun, adjective, or adverb. It can also be part of a verb phrase.

When an infinitive appears by itself, it is diagrammed like any single word doing the same job.

**Examples:**     Lydia refused to help.

In this sentence, *to help* answers the question, *"refused* what?" *To help* is the direct object, so here, the infinitive is doing a noun's job.

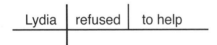

That was a day to remember.

*To remember* modifies the noun *day*; the infinitive is doing an adjective's job.

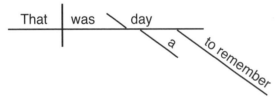

The senator rose to speak.

*To speak* modifies the verb *rose*; the infinitive is doing an adverb's job.

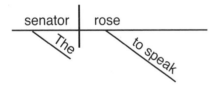

Working your way through The Process Chart will help you identify what job the infinitive is doing.

**Infinitive or preposition?**

Remember that, to be a preposition, a word must be in a prepositional phrase. That means there must be a noun acting as the object of a preposition. If the word to is followed by a verb, immediately think, "Infinitive!"

As with other verbals, sometimes an infinitive behaves like a verb, too. For example, it can take a direct object or be modified by an adverb. The infinitive and all of its modifiers and objects make up an **infinitive phrase.**

**Infinitive phrase**

An infinitive with all of its modifiers and objects acting as one unit is called an **infinitive phrase**.

Infinitive phrases are diagrammed in a special way, depending on whether they are acting as a noun or a modifier. The main diagramming structure you will use is a "broken dogleg." (Remember those from diagramming indirect objects?) Write *to* on the diagonal and the rest of the infinitive on the horizontal line. Then diagram any modifiers or objects as you normally would if the infinitive were the verb of a sentence.

**Example A:**     **When an infinitive phrase is a noun**

——*v*——  *pp*  *art*    *pn*     *lv adj*    *n*

To enlist (in the Navy) is his plan.

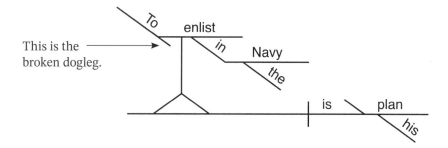

This is the broken dogleg.

When an infinitive is acting as a noun, the broken dogleg goes on a stilt above the space where that noun would ordinarily go. In this example, *To enlist in the Navy* is the subject, so the stilt goes in the subject spot and the broken dogleg goes on top of that. Infinitive phrases doing the job of a noun cannot be removed from a sentence without making it grammatically incorrect.

**Example B:**     **When an infinitive phrase is a modifier**

*pro*  *hv*     *av*    ——*v*——  *art*      *n*

We  are  going  to  see  the  parade.

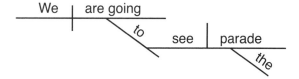

When an infinitive phrase is a modifier, the broken dogleg goes underneath the word it modifies. In this case, *to see the parade* is acting as an adverb, modifying the verb phrase *are going*. Like other modifiers, an infinitive phrase that is doing the job of a modifier can be removed from a sentence without making it grammatically incorrect.

**Example C:** **When an infinitive phrase has an understood *to***

Sometimes we don't use the whole infinitive. We leave off the *to*; when that happens, we say that the *to* is "understood."

> pn   av   v   art   n
>
> Dad helped bake the cake.

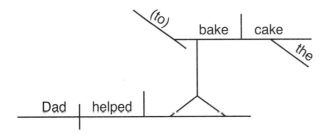

We still diagram the word *to* and put it on the diagram. We just put parentheses around it to show that it's "understood." This usage can be tricky to identify, so be careful and use your Process Chart! If you ask, in Step 6 of The Process, "Dad helped *who or what*?", the answer is the infinitive phrase *(to) bake the cake*. We need to add the word *to* to make it clear that *bake* is part of an infinitive.

**Example D:** **When an infinitive has a subject**

An infinitive is the only verbal that can have a subject. When it does, it is called an **infinitive clause** (we'll learn more about clauses in *Analytical Grammar: Punctuation & Usage*, Lessons 2–4). Here's how to diagram it:

> pro   av   pro   —v—   pro   pp   adj   n
>
> I wanted him to help me (with my algebra).

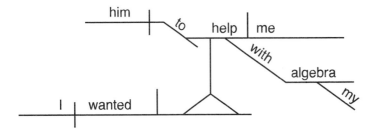

Whenever you see a noun or pronoun in front of an infinitive, always ask, "Is that noun or pronoun doing the **action** of the infinitive?" If the answer is yes, then the infinitive has a subject. (In other words, you have an infinitive clause.) In our example sentence, think about what I want. I want **help with my algebra!** I don't want **him**; **him** is not the direct object. I want him **to help**. **To help** is the direct object and **him** is the pronoun doing the action, so **to help** is an infinitive with a subject. Again, using the questions in The Process Chart will help you clarify what each part of speech is doing.

Now complete the **Infinitive** line on your Verbal Phrases chart. Be sure to fill in both jobs that an infinitive phrase can do: noun and modifier.

# Infinitive Phrases: Exercise A

**Directions**

Parse the sentences below and put parentheses around the prepositional phrases. Underline the infinitives and infinitive phrases. If the infinitive/infinitive phrase is doing a noun's job, write what that job is. If the infinitive/infinitive phrase is doing the job of a modifier, write the word or phrase being modified.

　　　　　　——v——　　n　　lv　art　adj　　　n

**1)**　To give advice is a simple matter.

　　　　*subject*


　　　　pro　hv　　av　　——v——　art　　n

**2)**　We were hoping to solve the puzzle.

　　　　*direct object*


　　　　　pn　　av　——v——

**3)**　James plans to go.

　　　　*direct object*


　　　　pro　av　pp　art　　n　　——v——　pp　　pro

**4)**　I went (to the library) to look (for him).

　　　　*went*


　　　　art　adj　　n　——v——　art　　n　　lv　——v——　pro

**5)**　The best way to keep a secret is to forget it.

　　　　*way; predicate nominative*

**Directions**

Parse the sentences below and put parentheses around the prepositional phrases. Underline the infinitives and infinitive phrases. Diagram the sentences. Use The Process Chart, the Verbal Phrases Chart, and your lesson notes if you need help.

       *pro     av  ——v——  art   n   pp  art   n*

**6)** They started to discuss the plans (for the dance).

       *pro  hv  av  art   n    ——v——*

**7)** I could feel the impulse to scream.

       *——v—— art adj   n   lv art   adj     n*

**8)** To be a good friend is an important thing.

       *pn  conj   pn     av    v   art   n*

**9)** Phil and Claude helped move the couch.

*See Example C in the lesson notes.*

       *art   n   lv   adj    ——v——*

**10)** The door is difficult to open.

# Infinitive Phrases: Exercise B

### Directions

Parse the sentences below and put parentheses around the prepositional phrases. Underline the infinitives and infinitive phrases. Be on the lookout for infinitives without *to*! Diagram the sentences. Use your Process Chart, the Verbal Phrases chart, and the lesson notes if you need help.

**Note:** These sentences may include other verbal phrases, but you only need to underline the infinitive phrases and infinitives.

*pro   av   —v—   adv   pp   n*
1) We hope to leave immediately (after school).

*pn   hv   adv   av   v   pro   art   adj   n*
2) Cathy did not dare tell us the bad news.

*pro   hv   av   —v—   art   n   v   pp   —pn—*
3) We are going to see the parade coming (down Main Street).

*Hint: The infinitive phrase "to see the parade coming down Main Street" contains a participial phrase acting as a modifier. It is modifying the word parade.*

*v   adj   n   pn   av   —v—   pro*
4) Hearing our footsteps, Fido ran to greet us.

*—v—   art   adj   n   av   art   adj   n*
5) To reach the fifth floor, take the other stairs.

*pp   v   adj   n   pro   av   —v—   art   n*
6) (After hearing her speech), I decided to become a doctor.

*hv   pro   av   pro   pp   v   art   n*
7) Have we done everything (except wash the dishes)?

*art   n   v   pp   art   n   av   v   adj   n*
8) The man digging (in the quarry) helped find our baseball.

*art   n   v  pp art     n       av ——v— art  adj    n*

**9)** The kids living (in the neighborhood) want to start a softball team.

*pro lv    adv      adj     ——v—— pp    n*

**10)** It is sometimes embarrassing to ask (for directions).

**Directions**

Write what job the following words are doing in each sentence. Choose your answers from among the following:

|  |  |  |
|---|---|---|
| **subject** | **object of the preposition** | **verb** |
| **modifier** | **direct object** | **indirect object** |
| **predicate nominative** | **predicate adjective** |  |

| Sentence # | Word | Job |
|---|---|---|
| 1 | immediately | *modifier* |
| 2 | tell us the bad news | *direct object* |
| 3 | parade | *direct object* |
| 4 | Hearing our footsteps | *modifier* |
| 5 | stairs | *direct object* |
| 6 | hearing her speech | *object of the preposition* |
| 7 | everything | *direct object* |
| 8 | baseball | *direct object* |
| 9 | to start a softball team | *direct object* |
| 10 | embarrassing | *predicate adjective* |

# Infinitive Phrases: Exercise C

**Directions**

Parse the sentences below and put parentheses around the prepositional phrases. Underline the infinitives, infinitive phrases, and infinitive clauses. (Some sentences include other kinds of verbals and verbal phrases.) Diagram the sentences. Use The Process Chart, the Verbal Phrases Chart, and your lesson notes if you need help.

**Note**: Sentences 3, 6, 8 and 10 contain infinitive clauses! That means the infinitive has a subject (that is not the subject of the entire sentence). Look back at Example D in your lesson notes to remind you how to diagram an infinitive clause.

     *n*       *av*    *pp*  *adj*  *n or v\**  *hv*  *adv*   *av*   ——*v*——  *art*    *n*

1)  Persons untrained (in scuba diving) are not allowed to demonstrate the equipment.

    *\*As long as your student recognizes diving as a gerund doing the noun job, they may mark it with either* **n** *or* **v**.

    ——*v*——   *n*    *av*  *art* *adj*    *n*

2)  To write poetry requires a good vocabulary.

    *pro* *hv*   *av*    *pn* ——*v*—— *adj*   *n*

3)  We are helping Bob to paint his house.

    *pro* *hv*   *av*    ——*v*——   *n*    *v*    *n*

4)  We are learning to diagram sentences containing phrases.

    ——*v*—— *art*  *n*    *v*   *pp* *pro* *lv*   *adj*

5)  To interrupt a person speaking (to you) is impolite.

    *pro*  *av*  *art* *n* ——*v*——  *adj*  *n*  *pp*   *n*

6)  We needed the vet to see Prince's leg (at once).

    *pro* *lv* *art*   *n*   ——*v*——  *pp*  *art*  *n*    *v*   *pp* *art*   *n*

7)  She is the person to see (about the job) advertised (in the paper).

    *hv*  *pro*  *av* *art*  *n*   *v*  *adj*   *n*

8)  Did you see the center foul our man?

              *pro    lv    adj   —v—   adj    n     v     pp   art    n*
**9)** They were glad to hear his voice coming (over the phone).


              *pn   hv   adv  av  pro   v        adv       pp      n*
**10)** Mom will not let us swim immediately (after lunch).


**Directions**

Write what job the following words are doing in each sentence. Choose your answers from among the following:

| *subject* | *object of the preposition* | *verb* |
|:---:|:---:|:---:|
| *modifier* | *direct object* | *indirect object* |
| *predicate nominative* | *predicate adjective* | |

| Sentence # | Word | Job |
|:---:|:---:|:---:|
| 1 | untrained in scuba diving | *modifier* |
| 2 | To write poetry | *subject* |
| 3 | Bob | *subject* |
| 4 | phrases | *direct object* |
| 5 | speaking to you | *modifier* |
| 6 | the vet to see Prince's leg at once | *direct object* |
| 7 | advertised in the paper | *modifier* |
| 8 | man | *direct object* |
| 9 | glad | *predicate adjective* |
| 10 | lunch | *object of the preposition* |

# Application & Enrichment

### Verb Tenses: Present Progressive and Past Progressive

The **progressive tense** is used to show action that **progresses** or **continues** (you may even hear it called the *continuous tense*). Verbs in the progressive tense indicate that the action occurred over a period of time.

**Present progressive tense** shows action that started in the past but is continuing right now. It is formed by using the correct present-tense form of **to be** plus the present participle (ending with -*ing*):

> I *am training* for a half marathon. (I started training in the past, and I am still training today.)

> The cat *is getting* chunky. (She started getting chunky in the past and is getting chunkier every day.)

**Past progressive tense** shows action that started in the past, continued for a time, and finished in the past. It is formed by using the correct past-tense form of **to be** plus the present participle (remember that the helping verb determines whether a verb is past, present, or future tense, not the participle):

> I *was training* for a half marathon. (I started training in the past, trained for a while, and then stopped. I'm not training anymore.)

> The cat *was getting* chunky. (She started getting chunkier, got chunkier for a while, but now she isn't getting any chunkier.)

Note that some verbs should not be used in the progressive tense! These are mostly verbs that describe a **state of being**, not an action. For example, the linking verbs we learned in Lesson 8 should not be used in the progressive tense. If a verb is describing what something *is* rather than what it *is doing*, don't use the progressive tense. Emotion verbs like *love, like, hate, want,* and *wish* should also not be used in the progressive:

> He wanted a piece of pizza. *not* He was wanting a piece of pizza.

> I love it. *not* I am loving it.

> It matters to you. *not* It is mattering to you.

In different areas of the United States, you may hear people use the progressive for these verbs, and that's fine in everyday speech. Like many other grammar guidelines that we don't follow on a regular basis, avoid using them in the progressive tense in formal writing or speech.

| *to walk* | present | past | future |
|---|---|---|---|
| **simple** | walk | walked | |
| **perfect** | have walked<br>have/has + past participle | had walked<br>had + past participle | |
| **progressive** | am walking<br>*am/are/is* +<br>present participle | was walking<br>*was/were* +<br>present participle | |
| **perfect progressive** | | | |

**Directions**

The sentences below have either present progressive tense or past progressive tense verbs. Circle the entire verb(s), then write the other progressive form of the verb below the sentence (if it's present progressive, write the past progressive verb; if it's past progressive, write the present progressive).

**Example:**    Laura (is studying) abroad for a semester.
was studying

1) Roadwork (is starting) on Highway 36 on Wednesday.
   *was starting*

2) The house (was standing) on a toxic waste dump.
   *is standing*

3) The game (is exciting,) with a tie score in the ninth inning!
   *was exciting*

4) I (am looking) for my phone while I (am holding) it.
   *was looking. was holding*

5) Juan and Jenny (were walking) toward the school.
   *are walking*

6) The squirrel (was living) dangerously, with its daring leaps and close calls with the cats!
   *is living*

7) The car's engine (is making) squealing noises.
   *was making*

8) The trees' leaves (were changing) to beautiful autumn colors.
   *are changing*

9) As long as I (am sitting) in the president's chair, we (are) not (enacting) that rule!
   *was sitting, were enacting*

10) The sound of the leaf blower (was driving) me mad.
    *is driving*

# Infinitive Phrases: Assessment

### Directions

Parse the sentences below and put prepositional phrases in parentheses. Underline the infinitives, infinitive phrases, and infinitive clauses. Diagram the sentences. Use The Process Chart, the Verbal Phrases Chart, and the lesson notes if you need help. Each correctly identified part of speech is worth one point; award one point for each correctly identified infinitive phrase or clause.

          *adj    n      av    pro  —v—  art    n*

___ **1)** My father helped me to wash the car.
<br>8

          *pn    hv   adv   av  —v— adv   pp       n*

___ **2)** Dad does not want to go out (after dinner).
<br>10

          *hv   pro   av      pn    v   adj    adj    n    *adv*

___ **3)** Did you hear Rochelle sing your favorite song yesterday?
<br>10

*\*In both the underlining and the diagramming, yesterday can either modify the verbal, sing, or the main verb, did hear. Count either one correct.*

          *pro hv    av       —v—  art   adj     n    v    adv  \*adv*

___ **4)** I am expecting to meet the six-o'clock train arriving here today.
<br>11

*\*In both the underlining and the diagramming, today can either modify the verbal, arriving, or the main verb, am expecting. Count either one correct.*

          *—v—  adj    n   lv  adj   adj    n    pp \*n or v pp     pn*

___ **5)** To see movie stars was our main motive (for going (to Hollywood)).
<br>14

*\*Students may mark the gerund going as either a noun or a verbal. Either is correct.*

          *pro lv adv     adj    pp art   adj     n  —v—  adv    adv*

___ **6)** It is often necessary (in a crowded bus) to step very carefully.
<br>13

          *art  adj    n    v    art  adj   n  hv   av   —v—   adj   pp art    n*

___ **7)** The young lady wearing the plaid coat is trying to look interested (in the game).
<br>16

          *hv   pro   av  art   n    v   adj      adj        n*

___ **8)** Did you see the team play their championship game?
<br>10

       *pn*    *av*   *pro* —*v*— *pp*  *art*   *adj*     *n*    *pp*     *n*

___ **9)** Jack dared us to walk (by the haunted house) (at midnight).
*13*

       *pn*     *av*   —*v*— *pro art adj*   *n*     *adv*      *v*    *pp*    *v*     *n*

___ **10)** Jim wanted to tell us a ghost story especially designed (for scaring people).
*14*

===
*119*

**Directions**

Write what job the following words are doing in each sentence. Choose your answers from among the following:

| subject | object of the preposition | verb |
|:---:|:---:|:---:|
| modifier | direct object | indirect object |
| predicate nominative | predicate adjective | |

*Five points each*

| Sentence # | Word | Job |
|:---:|:---:|:---:|
| 1 | me | *subject* |
| 2 | not | *modifier* |
| 2 | dinner | *object of the preposition* |
| 3 | yesterday | *modifier* |
| 4 | am expecting | *verb* |
| 4 | arriving here today | *modifier* |
| 5 | To see movie stars | *subject* |
| 5 | going to Hollywood | *object of the preposition* |
| 6 | It | *subject* |
| 6 | necessary | *predicate adjective* |
| 6 | very | *modifier* |
| 7 | wearing a plaid coat | *modifier* |
| 8 | you | *subject* |
| 8 | game | *direct object* |
| 9 | house | *object of the preposition* |
| 10 | us | *indirect object* |
| 10 | scaring people | *object of the preposition* |

## Diagrams

*Enter score from diagramming solutions here.*

$$\underline{\overline{\phantom{===}}}$$
104

$$\underline{\overline{\phantom{===}}} \textit{Total Points} \quad \frac{246}{308} = 80\%$$
308

# Appositive Phrases

## Instructor Notes

Students usually find appositives and appositive phrases quite easy, particularly after the challenge of identifying verbal phrases. The only issue may arise during the sentence-combining activity. Students may try to combine sentences using an adjective clause rather than an appositive phrase. Appositive phrases don't have a subject and verb (although they may have verbals). Here's an example of the correct way to combine two sentences using an appositive phrase:

Jake is my best friend.

He is going to math camp this summer.

Students may initially try to say something like, "Jake, who is my best friend, is going to math camp this summer." *Who is my best friend* is an adjective clause (which we will learn about in Lesson 5). Notice that it has a subject and verb: *who is*. These are not necessary if you are using an appositive phrase: "Jake, my best friend, is going to math camp this summer," or "My best friend, Jake, is going to math camp this summer." In both of these examples, the appositive is renaming the first noun.

*Diagramming solutions are found after Lesson 7.*

# Lesson 4: Appositive Phrases

Now let's talk about another kind of phrase—the appositive phrase. First we need to understand what an appositive is.

> **Appositive**
> An **appositive** is a noun or pronoun that restates or renames another noun or pronoun. The noun or pronoun is further identified or explained by the appositive. Usually the appositive follows the noun or pronoun it renames.

You will usually find appositives within an appositive phrase.

**Appositive phrases**

An **appositive phrase** is an appositive and any modifiers that work together as a unit to restate a noun or pronoun.

**Example 1:**     Jimmy, <u>a star athlete</u>, will surely get a sports scholarship to college.


*A star athlete* restates who *Jimmy* is. It tells more about him.

**Example 2:**     <u>A man of integrity</u>, Mr. Aldritch never cheats anyone.


Sometimes the appositive or appositive phrase comes before the noun being restated. *A man of integrity* is another name for *Mr. Aldritch* even though it comes before his name in the sentence.

One helpful clue to identifying appositives and appositive phrases is that they are usually set apart from the noun or pronoun they are restating with commas.

Appositive phrases are very useful in our writing to combine two shorter, more boring sentences into one longer, more interesting one:

$$pn \quad lv \quad adj \quad adj \qquad n$$

**Example 3:**     Jake  is  my  best  friend.

$$pro \quad hv \quad av \quad pp \quad adj \qquad n \qquad adj \qquad n$$

He  is  going  (to  math  camp)  this  summer.

We can combine these sentences because Jake is the topic of both of them. Here are two different ways to place an appositive phrase in a combined sentence:

$$pn \qquad adj \quad adj \qquad n \quad hv \quad av \quad pp \quad adj \qquad n \qquad adj \qquad n$$

Jake, <u>my  best  friend</u>,  is  going  (to  math  camp)  this  summer.

$$adj \quad adj \qquad n \qquad pn \quad hv \quad av \quad pp \quad adj \qquad n \qquad adj \qquad n$$

My  best  friend,  <u>Jake</u>,  is  going  (to  math  camp)  this  summer.

Notice that in the second sentence, *My best friend* is the subject and *Jake* becomes the appositive. That's okay, because they are equals and therefore interchangeable!

*Jake = my best friend*

*my best friend = Jake*

If you intend to use appositives or appositive phrases in your writing, make sure that you don't accidentally make adjective clauses. **Phrases** don't have a subject and a verb; **clauses** do.

Here's an example of how you could combine the sentences to include an adjective clause:

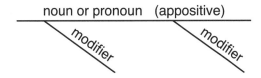

Jake, who is my best friend, is going (to math camp) this summer.

*Who is my best friend* is a **clause**, not a **phrase**, because it has a subject (*who*) and a verb (*is*). An appositive phrase may include a verbal, but it will never have a main verb with a subject. Watch out for this when you are combining sentences using an appositive phrase.

Diagramming an appositive or appositive phrase is simple: put the appositive in parentheses right after the noun or pronoun it is restating. Add any modifiers below the word they are modifying. If the modifier is describing the main noun or pronoun, it should be attached there. If it's describing the appositive, it should be attached there. It will look like this:

noun or pronoun   (appositive)
*modifier*              *modifier*

**Example 4:**

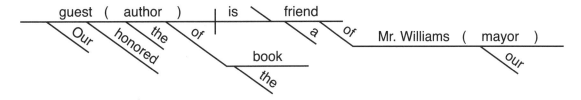

Our honored guest, the author (of the book), is a friend (of Mr. Williams), our mayor.

Any noun doing any job in a sentence can have an appositive. In this sentence, both the subject and one of the objects of the preposition have one. Good writing involves communicating information to the reader in an efficient, clear way, and appositives and appositive phrases can help you do exactly that.

# Appositive Phrases: Exercise A

**Directions**

Using an appositive or appositive phrase, combine each pair of sentences into one sentence. Make sure not to accidentally use an adjective clause instead! Remember that an appositive phrase cannot have a subject or verb.

*Answers may vary, but be sure to check that your student has used an appositive phrase, not an adjective clause (there should be no verb or subject). Possible answers are given below.*

1) Pumpkin is my cat.
   She is orange and round like a real pumpkin.

   *Pumpkin, my cat, is orange and round like a real pumpkin.*

2) She likes her toy.
   It is a catnip mouse.

   *She likes her toy, a catnip mouse.*

3) Cats are hunters by nature.
   They like toys that simulate prey.

   *Cats, hunters by nature, like toys that simulate prey.*

4) Pumpkin likes to sleep in her bed.
   Her bed is a hammock that hangs in the window.

   *Pumpkin likes to sleep in her bed, a hammock that hangs in the window.*

**Directions**

Parse the sentences below and put parentheses around the prepositional phrases. Underline the appositives and appositive phrases. Below each sentence, identify the appositive and the noun or pronoun that it is restating.

*Note: If your student includes modifiers in their answer, it should still be counted correct as long as their answer identifies the noun/pronoun and its appositive.*

     *adj*     *n*    *av*   *art*   *adj*    *n*    *art*  ——*pn*——

**5)** Our school has a drama club, the Thespian Society.

       *Thespian Society = club*

    ——*pn*——   *art*    *adj*     *n*    *lv*   *art*   *adj*    *n*

**6)** Mrs. Peng, an English teacher, is the club sponsor.

       *teacher = Mrs. Peng*

    *n*    *pp*   *art*   *n*    *adj*      *n*      *av*   *art*    *n*    *pp*   *art*   *adj*     *n*

**7)** Officers (of the club), mostly upperclassmen, planned a program (for the next assembly).

       *underclassmen = Officers*

   *art*     *n*    *hv*     *av*     *pp*    *pn*    *art*   *n*   *pp*   *adj*   *adj*      *n*

**8)** The program was presented (on Tuesday, the day of our weekly meeting).

       *day = Tuesday*

   ——*pn*——   *art*    *adj*     *n*     *av*     ——*pn*——     *n*    *pp*   *art*   *adj*

**9)** Jim Carson, the program chair, introduced Julia Hernandez, director (of the city's

     *adj*       *n*

repertory company).

       *chair = Jim Carson, director = Julia Hernandez*

   *pp*   ——*pn*——    *n*    *pp*   *art*  ——*pn*——   ——*pn*——    *av*    *adj*    *n*

**10)** From Nina Mason, president (of the Thespian Society), Ms. Hernandez received our award

    *pp*    *n*   *art*    *n*     *v*    *pp*   *adj*     *n*

(of merit), a plaque designed (by club members).

       *president = Nina Mason, plaque = award*

# Appositive Phrases: Exercise B

**Directions**

Parse the sentences below and put prepositional phrases in parentheses. Underline the appositives and appositive phrases. Diagram the sentences. Use The Process Chart and your lesson notes if you need help.

```
    pn    adj   adj    n     adv   av    v      adj     n
```
**1)** Jason, <u>my little nephew</u>, still enjoys hearing nursery rhymes.

```
   adj   n   ——pn——   hv   av  pro   pp     v     pp    pn
```
**2)** My friend, <u>Mary Jo</u>, will visit us (before leaving) (for Europe).

```
    ——pn——   art   n   pp  art  ——adj——   n    lv  art  adj   n    pp   adj     n
```
**3)** Carolyn Keene, <u>the author (of the Nancy Drew stories)</u>, is a popular writer (with young people)

```
     v     pp    n
```
interested (in mysteries).

```
   hv   pro   av   ——pn——    adj  adj    n
```
**4)** Have you met Marie Ritterman, <u>my best friend</u>?

**Directions**

Write what job the following words are doing in each sentence. Choose your answers from among the following:

| subject | object of the preposition | verb |
| :---: | :---: | :---: |
| modifier | direct object | indirect object |
| predicate nominative | predicate adjective | |

| Sentence # | Word | Job |
| :---: | :---: | :---: |
| 1 | hearing nursery rhymes | *direct object* |
| 2 | will visit | *verb* |
| 3 | writer | *predicate nominative* |
| 4 | best | *modifier* |

**Directions**

The following sentences all have appositive phrases. Underline the appositive phrase, then rewrite the sentence as two separate sentences. Use all of the words from the original sentence and add additional words where necessary.

*Answers may vary.*

**5)** Science, <u>my favorite class this year</u>, gets more fascinating with each month.

> *Science is my favorite class this year.*
> *It gets more fascinating with each month.*

**6)** The Randolph twins, <u>members of the track team</u>, have to report for practice soon.

> *The Randolph twins are members of the track team.*
> *They have to report for practice soon.*

**7)** Archimedes, <u>a Greek physicist</u>, supposedly made one of his discoveries in the bathtub.

> *Archimedes was a Greek physicist.*
> *Supposedly, he made one of his discoveries in the bathtub.*

**8)** At night the old house made strange noises, <u>sounds like footsteps or voices</u>.

> *At night the old house made strange noises.*
> *The noises were sounds like footsteps or voices.*

**9)** Bands became famous when they appeared on "American Bandstand," <u>a television show with live music and dancing teenagers</u>.

> *Bands became famous when they appeared on "American Bandstand."*
> *"American Bandstand" was a television show with live music and dancing teenagers.*

# Appositive Phrases: Exercise C

**Directions**

Using an appositive phrase, combine the two sentences into one.

*Answers will vary. Example solutions are given.*

**1)** *Little Women* is a favorite book for young people.
It was considered an absolutely necessary part of my education.

> *Little Women, a favorite book for young people, was considered an absolutely necessary part of my education.*

**2)** Mr. Chang is my geography teacher.
He once visited indigenous people living deep in the jungles of the Amazon Valley.

> *Mr. Chang, my geography teacher, once visited indigenous people living deep in the jungles of the Amazon Valley.*

**3)** Catching a sailfish is my uncle's lifelong dream.
Catching a sailfish is the goal of many fishermen.

> *Catching a sailfish, my uncle's lifelong dream, is the goal of many fishermen.*

**Directions**

Parse the sentences below and put prepositional phrases in parentheses. Underline the appositives and appositive phrases. Diagram the sentences. Use The Process Chart and your lesson notes if you need help.

```
        art   n     v    adv  adv   av  —v— pp  adj  n   art     adj    adj    n
```

**4)** The boy living next door loved to work (on his car), a dilapidated old wreck.

> *The phrase* next door *might cause some confusion. Because these words modify the verbal* living, *both words are acting as adverbs.*

```
        pro  pp  art    n    art   n  conj art  n    hv    av    pp  art  n     v
```

**5)** Both (of the animals), a horse and a cow, were saved (from the fire) started

```
        pp       n
```
(by lightning).

Diagramming a compound appositive is something new and there is not really a "right" way to do it (since it rarely happens!), so you are free to be creative. After you have tried it, ask your instructor to show you how we chose to do it.

```
        art adj      adj      n   art  n  pp art   n      av   art   n   —v— pp  art   n
```

**6)** A black funnel-shaped cloud, the sign (of a tornado), forced the family to hide (in the cellar).

**Directions**

Write what job the following words are doing in each sentence. Choose your answers from among the following:

| | | |
|---|---|---|
| *subject* | *object of the preposition* | *verb* |
| *modifier* | *direct object* | *indirect object* |
| *predicate nominative* | *predicate adjective* | |

| Sentence # | Word | Job |
|---|---|---|
| 4 | living next door | *modifier* |
| 5 | Both | *subject* |
| 5 | lightning | *object of the preposition* |
| 6 | family | *subject* |

# Application & Enrichment

### Verb Tenses: Present/Past Perfect Progressive Tense

| *to walk* | present | past | future |
|---|---|---|---|
| **simple** | walk | walked | |
| **perfect** | have walked<br>*have/has* + past participle | had walked<br>*had* + past participle | |
| **progressive** | am walking<br>*am/are/is* +<br>present participle | was walking<br>*was/were* +<br>present participle | |
| **perfect progressive** | have been walking<br>*have/has been* +<br>present participle | had been walking<br>*had been* +<br>present participle | |

Another English verb tense is the **perfect progressive tense**, sometimes called the **perfect continuous tense**. As you can probably tell, it is a combination of the two previous tenses (perfect tense and progressive tense). We know that, in grammar, **perfect** means *completed* and **progressive** means *continuing*. That seems like an impossible combination, doesn't it? But it's really not. Use perfect progressive tense when the focus is on the action itself, not the result of the action. Look at the examples below for more details.

### Present perfect tense

I have read all of that author's books. (The focus is on *books*, not the action *have read*. The reading is completed; the books are finished being read.)

### Present perfect progressive tense

I have been reading all of that author's books. (The focus is on the action *have been reading*. The reading was begun in the past and is continuing today. The books are still being read.)

The **present perfect progressive tense** focuses on an action that began in the past and continues to the present, usually showing a duration of time and focusing on the action, not the result. It is formed with the correct present perfect form of ***to be (have/has been) + the present participle (ending in –ing)***. It can be used to show the following:

- a new or temporary continuous action
  I've been eating a lot of salads recently. (*I used to not eat many salads, but recently I have been eating a lot of them.*)
  I have been getting a lot of calls about my car's extended warranty. (*Getting these calls is a new thing and I continue to get them. Hopefully it is temporary!*)

- an emphasis on the duration of the time an action has been continuing into the present
  He has been working on the car for six months. (*He started working on the car six months ago and hasn't finished working on it yet.*) Compare this to:
  He had worked on the car for six months.

- an action that is the result of another completed action
  I've been jogging, so I am all sweaty. (*I'm sweaty **because** I've been jogging.*)
  Juan has been snacking all afternoon; that's why he's not hungry. (*Juan's not hungry **because** he's been snacking all afternoon.*)

The **past perfect progressive tense** also shows a continuous action, but one that starts and is completed in the past over a duration of time. It is formed with the past perfect form of *to be* (**had been**) + **the present participle (ending in –*ing*).**

It can be used to show a relationship to another past action that occurred while the past perfect progressive action was happening.

**Example:**     I ***had been Christmas shopping*** when my car ***ran*** out of gas.

                              past perfect progressive                    past tense

It can also show an action that has an effect on another action:

**Example:**     Dad ***was tired*** because the baby ***had***n't ***been sleeping*** well.

                              past tense                         past perfect progressive

The perfect progressive tense is often used with signal words—adverbs or other words indicating time or sequence—that emphasize the passage of time. Look for words like *when, whenever, before, after, recently, lately*; or a duration of time, like *six months*.

**Directions**

Circle the verb or verb phrase(s). Identify what form of the verb is used. Write the number(s) for the correct answer in the blank next to the sentence. Use the following numbers:

| | |
|---|---|
| **A)** present tense | **E)** present progressive |
| **B)** past tense | **F)** past progressive |
| **C)** present perfect | **G)** present perfect progressive |
| **D)** past perfect | **H)** past perfect progressive |

*H, B* **1)** The manager (had been hoping) to hire the applicant, but she (accepted) another job.

*E, A* **2)** Jenna and I (are planning) to go to the concert if we (have) enough money.

*C* **3)** I (have) already (given) my answer to that question.

*F, B* **4)** We (were planning) to jump off of the bus as soon as it (stopped.)

*C* **5)** Everett and Josh (have met) before.

*G* **6)** I (have been waiting) my whole life to attend a ballgame at Wrigley Field!

*H, B* **7)** The old house (had) not (been maintained) well, but the new owner (was) determined to fix it up.

*E* **8)** The gloomy weather (is making) me feel quite blue.

*B* **9)** Through the window, we (saw) a lovely, plump, orange cat basking on the windowsill.

*E* **10)** The girls (are planning) to play cards all night at the sleepover.

# Appositive Phrases: Assessment

**Directions**

Parse the following sentences and put the prepositional phrases in parentheses. Underline the appositives and appositive phrases. Diagram the sentences. Use The Process Chart and your lesson notes if you need help.

*Each correctly parsed part of speech is worth one point, including prepositional phrases and underlining the appositive phrase.*

      ————pn———      art    n    pp   adj   adj    ————pn————    av    n

__ **1)** *Gone with the Wind,* the winner (of several 1939 Academy Awards), causes concern
15

     pp     adj     n

(among modern viewers).

    art  n  art  n  pp art  ——pn——    av    art   adj   adj    n   pp art

__ **2)** The story, a tale (of the Civil War), romanticizes the horrific slave culture (of the
19

     adj     pn

American South).

    art   adj   adj    n    ————pn————   lv art   adj    adj    adj    n

__ **3)** The story's main character, Scarlett O'Hara, is a beautiful, spoiled southern belle
17

    v    pp art    n

living (on a plantation).

    art  ——pn——  adj   adj    n   ——v—— art    n    av   adv  conj   av

__ **4)** The Civil War, that crucial struggle to free the slaves, comes along and destroys
19

     adj     adj    n  pp  n

Scarlett's privileged way (of life).

     adj   n   pn  hv    av   conj   pn    av   ——v—— adj    n

__ **5)** Her home, Tara, is destroyed, and Scarlett struggles to feed her household.
12

═══
82

**Directions**

Combine the following sentences into one sentence using an appositive phrase. Make sure to include all of the information in the original sentences in your new sentence.

*Answers will vary. Each sentence is worth five points if the new sentence:*

- *properly combines the sentences by using an appositive phrase;*

- *provides all of the information in the original sentences.*

*An example of one possible answer is provided.*

___
5   **6)** Mammy and Pork are former slaves.
      Scarlett counts them as part of her family.

> *Scarlett counts Mammy and Pork, former slaves, as part of her family.*

___
5   **7)** Mammy is Scarlett's former nursemaid.
      She is the most likable character in the film.

> *Mammy, Scarlett's former nursemaid, is the most likable character in the film.*

___
5   **8)** Scarlett is a born Southerner.
      Scarlett never condemns the cruel and unjust institution of slavery.

> *Scarlett, a born Southerner, never condemns the cruel and unjust institution of slavery.*

___
5   **9)** Hattie McDaniel is the actor portraying Mammy in the film.
      She skillfully demonstrates her character's wisdom and morality.

> *Hattie McDaniel, the actor portraying Mammy in the film, skillfully demonstrates her character's wisdom and morality.*

___
5   **10)** McDaniel won the award for Best Supporting Actress in 1939 for her role.
      She was the first Black Oscar winner.

> *McDaniel, the first Black Oscar winner, won the award for Best Supporting Actress in 1939 for her role.*

___
25

**Directions**

Write what job the following words are doing in each sentence. Choose your answers from among the following:

| subject | object of the preposition | verb |
| modifier | direct object | indirect object |
| predicate nominative | predicate adjective | |

*Five points each*

| Sentence # | Word | Job |
|:---:|:---:|:---:|
| 1 | concern | *direct object* |
| 2 | Civil War | *object of the preposition* |
| 2 | American | *modifier* |
| 3 | belle | *predicate nominative* |
| 3 | living | *modifier* |
| 4 | way | *direct object* |
| 5 | Scarlett | *subject* |
| 5 | to feed | *modifier* |
| 5 | household | *direct object* |

$\overline{\overline{\phantom{45}}}$
*45*

**Diagrams**

*Enter score from diagramming solutions here.*

$\overline{\overline{\phantom{66}}}$
*66*

$\overline{\overline{\phantom{218}}}$ *Total Points* $\dfrac{174}{218} = 80\%$
*218*

# Lesson 5
# Adjective Clauses

## Instructor Notes

This lesson will introduce students to clauses and the concept that all sentences are clauses, but not all clauses are sentences. Why, if there is a subject and a verb, can a clause not stand on its own? What makes it a dependent clause instead of an independent one? Students will learn to look for subordinate conjunctions and other signals to help them make this determination. The competent usage of independent clauses, dependent clauses, and phrases allows students to relate complex thoughts and concepts.

*Diagramming solutions are found after Lesson 7.*

# Lesson 5: Adjective Clauses

We've learned a lot about different kinds of phrases, groups of words that work together as a unit to do the job of a part of speech. (For example, can you find the appositive phrase in the previous sentence?) Another kind of word group that works together as a unit to communicate more complex thoughts is a **clause**. Before we get into adjective clauses, let's learn more about what makes clauses different from phrases.

> **Clauses**
> A **clause** is a group of words that *contains a verb and its subject* and is used as part of a sentence.

The key difference is that phrases **do not** include verbs (*verbals*, yes; *verbs*, no). If you see a group of words that you think might be a phrase, but you notice it includes a subject and verb, **it's a clause**.

Just like phrases, there are several different types of clauses that do the jobs of different parts of speech.

> **Independent clauses and sentences**
> If a clause expresses a complete thought, we call it an **independent clause.** Independent clauses can be attached to other clauses. A **sentence** is a kind of independent clause that stands alone. To be considered a grammatically correct sentence, there must be at least one independent clause.

> **Subordinate clauses**
> Some clauses do not express a complete thought even though they have a subject and verb. These are called **subordinate clauses** and they must be attached to an independent clause. Subordinate clauses are sometimes called **dependent clauses**.

Subordinate clauses need independent clauses to complete their meaning.

> **Example 1:**     After it stopped raining, we played softball.

*After it stopped raining* has a subject (*it*) and a verb (*stopped*), so it is a clause. But it doesn't make any sense by itself. We're left thinking, "After it stopped raining, *what*?" It is a **subordinate clause** because it doesn't express a complete thought. We need more information!

*We played softball* is also a clause, with a subject (*we*) and verb (*played*). It is a complete thought. This **independent clause** could stand alone as a sentence. When we add the subordinate clause *After it stopped raining*, it is a stronger sentence because it gives us more context about **when** we played. Look at the following sentence and see if you can find the subordinate clause.

> **Examples:**     When the cat woke up, it walked daintily along the back of the couch toward its dinner.

What is the **independent clause** in this sentence?

> *it walked daintily along the back of the couch toward its dinner*

What is the **subordinate clause**?

> *When the cat woke up*

Now we have enough information to talk about **adjective clauses**.

### Adjective clauses

An **adjective clause** is a subordinate clause that modifies a noun or pronoun.

The easiest way to spot an adjective clause is to look at the **first word of the clause**. Adjective clauses are introduced by **relative pronouns**. Remember them from way back in *Grammar Basics*, Lesson 2?
Don't worry; here they are!

| Relative Pronouns | |
|---|---|
| who | |
| whom | use when referring to **people** |
| whose | |
| which | |
| that | use when referring to **things** |

You will need to be familiar enough with relative pronouns to recognize one when you see it, because they are the signals that tell you, "Hey! This is an adjective clause!"

The relative pronoun does two things at once. First, remember that it's still a pronoun, so it takes the place of, or relates to, the noun or pronoun in the independent clause that is being modified by the adjective clause. Second, it serves as a part of the clause. The relative pronoun could be the subject of the clause, a direct or indirect object, or the object of the preposition. Look at the following examples:

*pn*    *pro*  *av*  *pp*  *pn*    *adv*    *av*    *pn*

**Example 3:**    Yvette, <u>who lived (in France)</u>, quickly learned English.

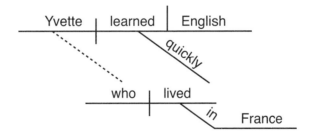

***Who** lived in France* is a subordinate clause that modifies the subject of the sentence, *Yvette*. The relative pronoun ***who*** 1) is the subject of the subordinate clause, and 2) stands for *Yvette* in the subordinate clause.

A subordinate clause is attached to the noun or pronoun it's modifying with a slanted, dashed line.

*art    n    pro    pro    av    adv    av    art    n*

**Example 4:**    The  man  whom  you  met  yesterday  bought  a  house.

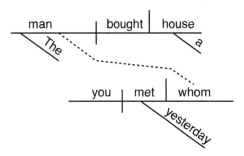

In this sentence, the subordinate clause, ***whom*** *you met yesterday,* is modifying *man.* We use ***whom*** because of the job the relative pronoun is doing in the clause. When we diagram the clause, we see that *you* is the subject and *met* is the verb. ***Who*** is one of the few words (mostly pronouns) in English that changes its case. ***Who,*** because it replaces the noun or pronoun that is the subject of the sentence, is a *subjective* pronoun. ***Whom*** is an *objective* pronoun. It can do the job of direct object, indirect object, or the object of the preposition. In this clause, it is a direct object.

*adj    n    pp    pro    pro    av    art    n    av    pro    art    n*

**Example 5:**    My  aunt,  (to  **whom**)  I  sent  a  gift,  wrote  me  a  letter.

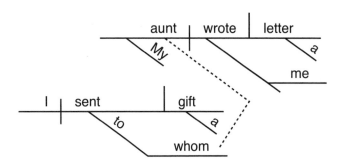

The subordinate clause *to **whom** I sent a gift* is modifying *aunt.* We use ***whom*** because it is the object of the preposition. You could also say:

My aunt, ***whom*** I sent a gift to, wrote me a letter. (It would be diagrammed in the same way.)

Older grammar texts taught that it was wrong to end a sentence or clause with a preposition, but it's now understood that it's not wrong in English (only in Latin). Sometimes, trying to move the preposition so it's not at the end of the sentence or clause can make a really awkward sentence, so a preposition is okay to end a sentence *with* (see what we did there?).

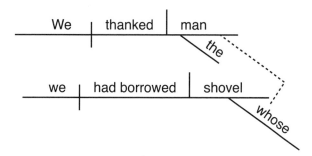

**Example 6:**     We thanked the man whose shovel we had borrowed.

*Whose* is a possessive form of **who** that is used to show that something belongs to **who**. It can be parsed as either an adjective or a pronoun, because it's acting as a modifier in the subordinate clause. Don't confuse it with **who's**, which is a contraction of **who is**. Read on for some helpful tips on knowing what word to use when!

**Who, Whom, Whose, and Who's – Huh?**

These are words that are frequently confused. The first three are relative pronouns. The fourth is a contraction. They are all used to talk about **people**, not things. Here's your guide to which to use when:

**Who**   This relative pronoun can only stand in for nouns or pronouns that are the **subject** of the sentence. This is an easy one to remember because it's the one we use the most in English! Because it's the subject, you may hear it referred to as the **subjective** case. It's also known as the **nominative** case.

**Whom**   This one is a little trickier to many English speakers, but not for you! You know all about objects: direct objects, indirect objects, and objects of the preposition. **Whom** is used to replace a noun or pronoun that is doing the job of an **object**. That's why it is called the **objective** case. Most people don't bother with **whom** when they are speaking even though it is technically correct. However, if you want to really impress your English teacher, using **whom** correctly is a great way to do that!

**Whose**   Besides being a relative pronoun, **whose** is a **possessive** pronoun that means "belonging to whom?" *Whose shoes are these in the middle of the hallway?* Yikes! I hope they're not yours!

**Who's**   This word is commonly confused with **whose** because we know that the way to make most words possessive is to add apostrophe *s*. However, as we see above, we already have a word that means that: **whose**. The other thing we use apostrophes for is to show when we've left letters out to make a contraction. **Who's** is the contraction for **who is**. We already know when **who** can be used. If you can replace *who's* with *who is* in your sentence, then it's the correct word to use.

**Example:**   **Who's** riding the blue bike today?
**Who is** riding the blue bike today?

That makes sense! **Who's** is the correct word.

**Who's** is the blue bike?
**Who is** is the blue bike?

Nope, that doesn't make sense. Use **whose** to show possession.

Correct: **Whose** is the blue bike?

# Adjective Clauses: Exercise A

### Directions

In each sentence below, underline the subordinate clause. Each of the clauses is an adjective clause. Write the relative pronoun and what the adjective clause is modifying below the sentence.

1) The Theodore Roosevelt museum has been established in the house <u>in which Roosevelt was born</u>.

   *which; modifies* house

2) It is located on the basement floor of Roosevelt's birthplace, <u>which is on East Twentieth Street</u>.

   *which; modifies* birthplace

3) The museum contains books, letters, and documents <u>that pertain to Roosevelt's public life</u>.

   *that; modifies books*, letters, and documents

4) There is an exercise bike <u>that Roosevelt used during his time at the White House</u>.

   *that; modifies* bike

5) During the war he led the Rough Riders, <u>who made the charge up San Juan Hill</u>.

   *who; modifies* Rough Riders

# Adjective Clauses: Exercise B

**Directions**

Parse the sentences below and put parentheses around the prepositional phrases. Underline the subordinate clause and circle the relative pronoun. Diagram the entire sentence. Use The Process Chart and your notes if you need help.

  ——pn——   *av*   *art*  *n*  *pro pro hv*  *av*

**1)** Mrs. Dalton recommended the movie (that) I am seeing.

  *adv av art*  *n*  *pro pro*  *av*  *pp*  *pro*

**2)** Here is the letter (that) I wrote (to you).

   *n*  *pro*  *av* ——*v*——  *n*   *hv*  *av*  *adv*  *adv*

**3)** People (who) want to learn languages must study every day.

   *n*  *pro*  *av art adj*  *n*  *adv*  *av*  *adv*

**4)** Students (who) read a great deal usually write well.

  *pro*  *pp art*   *n*   *pro*  *hv*  *av*  *pp*   *n*   *av*  *pp adj*   *n*

**5)** Some (of the paintings) (that) were done (by students) sold (for big money)!

   *pn*  *pro*  *lv*  *art*   *n*  *pp art*  *adj*   *n*  *av*   *adj*   *n*

**6)** Mercury, (who) was the messenger (of the Roman gods), wore winged sandals.

  *art*  *n*  *pro*  *art*   *n*  *av*  *lv* ——*pn*—— *art adj*   *n*

**7)** The man (whom) the policeman wants is Jake the Snake, a petty thief.

  *hv*  *art*   *n*  *pro/adj*  *n*  *lv adj*  *adv*  *av*  *pp art*   *n*

**8)** Will the person (whose) lights are on please report (to the desk)?

  *art*  *n*  *pro*  *av*  *pro*  *pp art*  *n*  *hv*  *adv*  *av*  *art*   *n*

**9)** A person (who) knows nothing (about a topic) should not express an opinion.

  *pro lv art*  *n*  *pp*  *pro pro*  *av*  *art*  *n*

**10)** He is the man (from (whom) I bought the car).

**Directions**

Write what job the following words are doing in each sentence. Choose your answers from among the following:

| subject | object of the preposition | verb |
|:---:|:---:|:---:|
| modifier | direct object | indirect object |
| predicate nominative | predicate adjective | |

| Sentence # | Word | Job |
|:---:|:---:|:---:|
| 1 | that | *direct object* |
| 2 | Here | *modifier* |
| 3 | languages | *direct object* |
| 4 | Students | *subject* |
| 5 | that | *subject* |
| 5 | money | *object of the preposition* |
| 6 | messenger | *predicate nominative* |
| 7 | whom | *direct object* |
| 8 | please | *modifier* |
| 9 | nothing | *direct object* |
| 9 | not | *modifier* |
| 10 | whom | *object of the preposition* |

## Adjective Clauses: Exercise C

**Directions**

Parse the sentences below and put parentheses around the prepositional phrases. Underline the subordinate clause and circle the relative pronoun. Diagram the entire sentence. Use The Process Chart and your notes if you need help.

   *pro av adv   pp  art   n   pro  ————pn————  av    adv*

**1)** I did well (on the test) (that) Mrs. Freeman gave yesterday.

   *adj   n   pro   av   adj    n   av   n   pp  adj    n*

**2)** My cousin, (who) enjoys practical jokes, put pepper (into my popcorn).

   *pn    av    pp  art   n   pp   pro  pro  av  adj   adj    n*

**3)** Dad disappeared (into the shed) (in (which)) he kept his gardening tools.

   *adj   n  pro/adj   adj    v    n   lv    adj   av   adj  adj    n*

**4)** My sister, (whose) horseback riding skills are amazing, won seven blue ribbons.

   *adj    n    pro   lv adv adj  pp pro  hv   av   pn*

**5)** This dress, (which) is too long (for you), may fit Mary.

**Directions**

Write what job the following words are doing in each sentence. Choose your answers from among the following:

subject          object of the preposition          verb

modifier          direct object          indirect object

predicate nominative          predicate adjective

| Sentence # | Word | Job |
|:---:|:---:|:---:|
| 1 | well | modifier |
| 1 | that | direct object |
| 2 | who | subject |
| 3 | which | object of the preposition |
| 4 | ribbons | direct object |
| 5 | long | predicate adjective |

**Directions**

The following pairs of sentences are short and choppy. Rewrite them and combine the two sentences into one sentence using **adjective clauses**. You may change words, add words, or delete words, but your new sentence must 1) contain all of the ideas that were in the original sentences and 2) contain an adjective clause. Remember that your adjective clause must contain a relative pronoun, a subject, and a verb; and it must modify a noun or pronoun.

*These answers will vary. Possible solutions are provided. Use your judgment, but be sure that your student has used an adjective clause.*

**6)** Morris drove the white convertible. The convertible led the parade.

*Morris drove the white convertible which led the parade.*
*The white convertible, which Morris drove, led the parade.*

**7)** Einstein did not do well in school. He was a genius.

*Einstein, who was a genius, did not do well in school.*
*Einstein, who did not do well in school, was a genius.*

**8)** I ordered this hamburger. It is cold.

*This hamburger that I ordered is cold.*

**9)** That man is my uncle. I have admired him for a long time.

*I have admired that man, who is my uncle, for a long time.*
*That man, whom I have admired for a long time, is my uncle.*

**10)** The policeman's badge is lost. He is retiring in three months.

*The policeman who lost his badge is retiring in three months.*
*The policeman who is retiring in three months lost his badge.*

# Application & Enrichment

### Verb tenses: Future tenses

Now that you know how to form all of the present and past tenses, the future tenses should be easy. The future has all of the same tenses as past and present.

| *to walk* | present | past | future |
|---|---|---|---|
| **simple** | walk | walked | will walk<br>*will* + root form<br>of the verb |
| **perfect** | have walked<br>*have/has* + past participle | had walked<br>*had* + past participle | will have walked<br>*will have* + past participle |
| **progressive** | am walking<br>*am/are/is* +<br>present participle | was walking<br>*was/were* +<br>present participle | will be walking<br>*will be* +<br>present participle |
| **perfect progressive** | have been walking<br>*have/has been* +<br>present participle | had been walking<br>*had been* +<br>present participle | will have been walking<br>*will have been* +<br>present participle |

Let's talk about each tense:

**Future (simple)** indicates an action that hasn't happened yet but will happen in the future. Add **will** to the root form of the verb (the infinitive without *to*) to form it.

> Tomorrow I **will clean** my house from top to bottom.
> Future generations **will** long **remember** what happened here.
> **Will** you **come** to my birthday party?

**Future perfect** indicates an action that isn't complete yet but will be completed by a certain point in the future. Add **will have** to the past participle of the verb.

> The party **will have started** before I can get there.
> If he gets one more, Jaden **will have collected** fifty vintage baseball cards.
> Morgen **will have entered** her name in the drawing by now.

**Future progressive** shows an action that will happen in the future for a period of time. Add **will be** to the present participle.

> Melissa **will be traveling** to the wedding.
> If he admits all that he has done wrong, he **will be talking** for a long time!
> Grandma and Granddad **will be coming** to stay at Christmas.

Finally, **future perfect progressive** shows that an ongoing action will continue for a certain amount of time at a point in the future. The action is not complete; it's expected to continue past the future point. It may have started in the past, present, or future. Using this tense usually indicates when the action will be completed. This tense is formed by adding **will have been** to the present participle.

> Next January, Linnea **will have been working** at her job for eight years.
> By the time I graduate, I **will have been attending** college for four and a half years.
> As of dinnertime, Juan **will have been playing** video games for three hours.

**Directions**

Write the future tenses of each verb in the spaces provided. Use the chart above if you need help.

| verb | simple future | future perfect | future progressive | future perfect progressive |
|---|---|---|---|---|
| swim | *will swim* | *will have swum* | *will be swimming* | *will have been swimming* |
| win | *will win* | *will have won* | *will be winning* | *will have been winning* |
| run | *will run* | *will have run* | *will be running* | *will have been running* |
| ask | *will ask* | *will have asked* | *will be asking* | *will have been asking* |
| demonstrate | *will demonstrate* | *will have demonstrated* | *will be demonstrating* | *will have been demonstrating* |

**Directions**

Write the indicated tense of each verb in the space provided. Use the chart above if you need help. Use ***they*** as your subject.

| | | |
|---|---|---|
| speak | past perfect | they *had spoken* |
| eat | present progressive | they *are eating* |
| show | future perfect | they *will have shown* |
| press | past progressive | they *were pressing* |
| shop | present perfect progressive | they *have been shopping* |
| write | present perfect | they *have written* |

# Adjective Clauses: Assessment

### Directions

Parse the sentences below and put parentheses around the prepositional phrases. Underline the subordinate clauses and circle the relative pronouns. Diagram the entire sentence. Use The Process Chart and your notes if you need help.

*Each correctly parsed part of speech is worth one point, including prepositional phrases, underlining the subordinate clause, and circling the relative pronoun.*

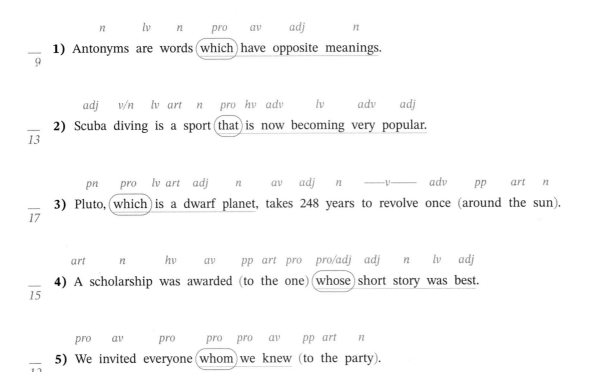

                     n      lv     n    pro     av    adj        n
__
 9   **1)** Antonyms  are  words (which) have  opposite  meanings.


             adj   v/n   lv  art   n   pro  hv  adv      lv       adv     adj
__
13   **2)** Scuba  diving  is  a  sport (that) is  now  becoming  very  popular.


             pn      pro   lv  art  adj    n     av   adj    n    ——v——   adv    pp    art   n
__
17   **3)** Pluto, (which) is  a  dwarf  planet,  takes  248  years  to  revolve  once (around  the  sun).


         art      n       hv     av     pp  art  pro  pro/adj  adj    n    lv   adj
__
15   **4)** A  scholarship  was  awarded (to  the  one) (whose) short  story  was  best.


         pro     av      pro      pro   pro   av   pp   art    n
__
12   **5)** We  invited  everyone (whom) we  knew (to  the  party).


═══
66

**Directions**

Write what job the following words are doing in each sentence. Choose your answers from among the following:

| subject | object of the preposition | verb |
|---------|---------------------------|------|
| modifier | direct object | indirect object |
| predicate nominative | predicate adjective | |

*Five points each*

| Sentence # | Word | Job |
|------------|------|-----|
| 1 | words | *predicate nominative* |
| 2 | popular | *predicate adjective* |
| 3 | 248 | *modifier* |
| 3 | sun | *object of the preposition* |
| 4 | whose | *modifier* |
| 5 | whom | *direct object* |

═══
*30*

**Directions**

The following pairs of sentences are short and choppy. Rewrite them and combine the two sentences into one sentence using an adjective clause. You may change words, add words, or delete words, but your sentence must 1) contain all of the ideas that were in the original sentences, and 2) contain an adjective clause. Remember: use **which** or **that** when referring to things and **who/whom/whose** when referring to people.

*Answers will vary. Check that your student's new sentence means the same thing as the original sentence and that they have used an adjective clause.*

*Two points each*

____ **6)** My cousin loves old movies. He stayed home this afternoon to watch TV.

*2*     *My cousin, who loves old movies, stayed home this afternoon to watch TV.*
       *My cousin, who stayed home this afternoon to watch TV, loves old movies.*

____ **7)** Dad built a "worm" fence. It has zigzagging rails.

*2*     *Dad built a "worm" fence that has zigzagging rails.*
       *The "worm" fence which Dad built has zigzagging rails.*

_____ **8)** The dress once belonged to my aunt. It has a poodle on the skirt.

    *2*         *The dress, which once belonged to my aunt, has a poodle on the skirt.*
                *The dress, which has a poodle on the skirt, once belonged to my aunt.*

_____ **9)** Johnny is too old to play with you. He wants to play with Jimmy.

    *2*         *Johnny, who is too old to play with you, wants to play with Jimmy.*
                *Johnny, who wants to play with Jimmy, is too old to play with you.*

_____ **10)** Mary wrote a book. It was on the bestseller list.

    *2*         *Mary wrote a book that was on the bestseller list.*
                *The book which Mary wrote was on the bestseller list.*

_____ **11)** I fell madly in love with the artist. He lives next door.

    *2*         *I fell madly in love with the artist who lives next door.*

_____ **12)** I stumbled over the scooter. It was lying on the sidewalk.

    *2*         *I stumbled over the scooter which was lying on the sidewalk.*
                *The scooter which I stumbled over was lying on the sidewalk*

_____ **13)** My father paid $100 for that chair. It once belonged to the mayor.

    *2*         *My father paid $100 for that chair, which once belonged to the mayor.*
                *That chair, which my father paid $100 for, once belonged to the mayor.*

_____ **14)** The little boy had lost his temper. He was screaming at his sister.

    *2*         *The little boy, who had lost his temper, was screaming at his sister.*
                *The little boy who was screaming at his sister had lost his temper.*

_____ **15)** That tall man coaches our football team. You met him yesterday.

    *2*         *Yesterday you met that tall man who coaches our football team.*
                *That tall man, whom you met yesterday, coaches our football team.*

=====
*20*

**Diagrams**
*Enter score from diagramming solutions here.*

=====
*59*

===== *Total Points*    $\dfrac{140}{175} = 80\%$
*175*

# Lesson 6
# Adverb Clauses

## Instructor Notes

Like adjective clauses, adverb clauses begin with signal words. Instead of relative pronouns, however, adverb clauses begin with a subordinating conjunction. Because of this conjunction, the subordinate clause can't stand on its own even though it has a subject and a verb. The subordinating conjunction signals to the reader, "This is only part of the information; read the rest of the sentence to find out!" The subordinating conjunction is only one indication that a clause is an adverb clause. The student will need to confirm that it is, in fact, modifying a verb to be sure.

As usual, the student is not required to memorize the list of subordinating conjunctions, but they do need to be familiar enough with them to question whether that is the job the word is doing and confirm it. Most subordinating conjunctions can also do other jobs, often that of a preposition. Students have the skills to confirm that they have an adverb clause with a subordinating conjunction and not some other part of speech or another kind of clause. Subordinating conjunctions are marked with *sc*.

*Diagramming solutions are found after Lesson 7.*

# Lesson 6: Adverb Clauses

Now that we've thoroughly discussed adjective clauses, it's time to talk about **adverb clauses**.

### Adverb clauses

An **adverb clause** is a group of words with a subject and a verb that modifies a verb, an adjective, or another adverb. It answers the questions "how?", "when?", "where?", or "why?" about one of those words in the independent clause.

**Example 1:**    Before the game started, we ate lunch.

The subordinate clause *Before the game started* tells you **when** we ate. It is an adverb clause modifying the verb *ate*.

**Example 2:**    I am glad that you are coming.

The subordinate clause *that you are coming* tells **why** I am glad. It is an adverb clause modifying the predicate adjective *glad*.

### How are adverb clauses different from adjective clauses?

First, as we've mentioned, adverb clauses modify verbs, adjectives, or adverbs, while adjective clauses modify nouns or pronouns. There are a couple of other clues you can use, as well:

1) Adverb clauses are introduced by **subordinating conjunctions**. You should become familiar enough with these words that you can recognize them as subordinating conjunctions when you see them in sentences.

| after | how | though |
|---|---|---|
| although | if | unless |
| as | in order that | until |
| as if | once | when |
| as long as | since | whenever |
| as soon as | so that | where |
| because | than | wherever |
| before | that | while |

*Note: these are not **all** of the subordinating conjunctions, just the most common ones. If you come across a word that's not on this list that you suspect to be a subordinating conjunction, you can use your grammar knowledge to identify it.*

When parsing a subordinating conjunction, mark it with *sc*.

You can see that several of these words can do other jobs besides being subordinating conjunctions. Many of them are prepositions, and we just learned in the last lesson that **that** can be a relative pronoun. These subordinating conjunctions are just a signal that there is a subordinate clause following. It's up to you and your grammar skills to identify what kind of clause it is. You will do that by identifying what word is being modified in the independent clause; that is, figuring out what question it is answering: *who, what, where, when, why,* or *how*.

**2)** Unlike the relative pronouns in adjective clauses, these subordinating conjunctions are **not a part of the little sentence included in the subordinate clause.** In adjective clauses, the relative pronoun is the subject, direct object, indirect object, object of the preposition, or a modifier in the subordinate clause. If it's removed from the clause, the clause no longer makes sense.

With an adverb clause, you can remove the subordinating conjunction, and you'll be left with a little mini-sentence that makes perfect sense on its own! Let's try this with our example sentences above:

**Example 1:**    Before the game started, we ate lunch.

Cover up the subordinating conjunction (*before*) with one thumb. Cover up the independent clause (*we ate lunch*) with the other thumb. The little sentence left over is *the game started*. That's a complete sentence on its own. It's the subordinating conjunction that makes it into a subordinate clause! Let's look at our other example sentence:

**Example 2:**    I am glad that you are coming.

When we cover up the independent clause *I am glad* and the subordinating conjunction *that*, we are left with *you are coming*. Again, that's a complete sentence! Use the Never-Fail Thumb Test whenever you're not sure if you have an adverb clause. If you have a little sentence left over after covering the subordinating conjunction and the independent clause, you know that it's an adverb clause! (This Thumb Test is especially useful when you have a word like **that**, which can do many different jobs in a sentence. If you can remove it and still have a little sentence, you will know that it's doing its subordinating conjunction job.)

### Diagramming sentences with adverb clauses

Just like with adjective clauses, the subordinate clause will be attached to the word it modifies with a dotted line. The difference is that you will put the subordinating conjunction on the dotted line.

|  | sc | art | n | av | art | n | pro | av | adj | n |
**Example 3:** Before the guests left the ballroom, they thanked their hosts.

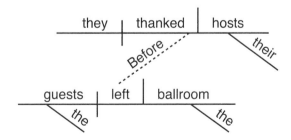

# Adverb Clauses: Exercise A

**Directions**

Parse the sentences below and put parentheses around the prepositional phrases. Mark subordinating conjunctions with **sc**. Underline the adverb clause. Diagram the sentences. Use The Process Chart and your lesson notes if you need help.

      *sc    art    n    av    pp  adj   n    pn    av   pro    adv*

**1)** Because the present came (from her aunt), Diane opened it immediately.

      *pro hv   av    art   n   sc pro  av   pp    n*

**2)** I will attend the party if it starts (by seven).

      *adj    n    av   adv   sc pro  av*

**3)** My brother slept later than I did.

      *sc    pro lv adv art  ——pn——  pro   av    v    adj      n*

**4)** Although I am not a Sherlock Holmes, I enjoy solving difficult puzzles.

      *pro  av  art    n    pp  art   n    sc  pro  hv    av    art     n*

**5)** He saw the author (of the play) when he was leaving the theater.

      *sc   pro  av  art   n   pp  art    n     av   pro  pp  adj    n*

**6)** After you add the eggs (to the mixture), beat it (for ten minutes).

      *pn   av   —sc— pro  hv   av   art    n*

**7)** John looked as if he had seen a ghost.

      *art    n     hv  adv  av  sc art     n     av  adv  adj    n  pp  pro*

**8)** The driveway will not set if the concrete has too much water (in it).

      *hv   pro  av  art    n    —sc—— pro hv  lv  art    adj      n*

**9)** Can you plan the party so that it will be a complete surprise?

      *sc   adj   n     av    adj   n   pro  hv  adv  av  pp  art     n*

**10)** Unless my dad changes his mind, I can not go (to the dance).

# Adverb Clauses: Exercise B

## Directions

Parse the sentences below and put parentheses around the prepositional phrases. Mark subordinating conjunctions with **sc**. Underline the adverb clauses. Diagram the sentences. Use The Process Chart and your lesson notes if you need help.

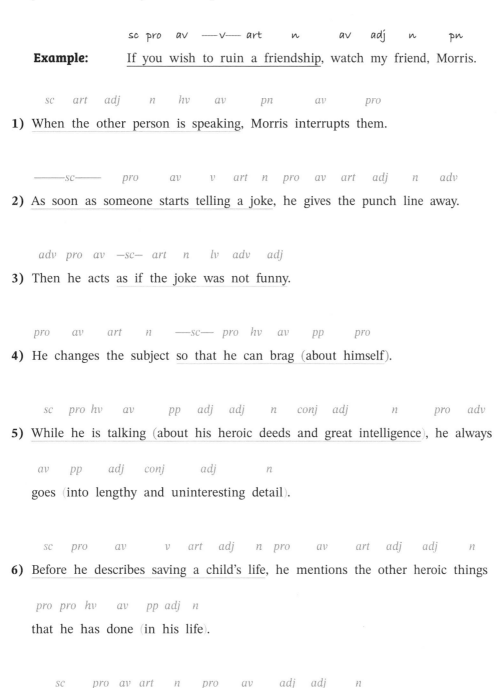

|  | sc | pro | av | —v— | art | n | av | adj | n | pn |
|--|----|-----|----|-----|-----|---|----|-----|---|----|
**Example:** If you wish to ruin a friendship, watch my friend, Morris.

          *sc   art   adj    n    hv    av    pn    av    pro*

**1)** When the other person is speaking, Morris interrupts them.

          *——sc——   pro    av    v   art  n  pro  av  art  adj   n   adv*

**2)** As soon as someone starts telling a joke, he gives the punch line away.

          *adv  pro  av  —sc—  art   n   lv   adv   adj*

**3)** Then he acts as if the joke was not funny.

          *pro   av   art   n   —sc—  pro  hv  av   pp    pro*

**4)** He changes the subject so that he can brag (about himself).

          *sc   pro  hv   av    pp   adj   adj    n   conj  adj      n    pro  adv*

**5)** While he is talking (about his heroic deeds and great intelligence), he always

          *av   pp   adj   conj    adj      n*

goes (into lengthy and uninteresting detail).

          *sc   pro    av    v   art  adj   n  pro    av    art   adj   adj     n*

**6)** Before he describes saving a child's life, he mentions the other heroic things

          *pro  pro  hv    av    pp  adj  n*

that he has done (in his life).

          *sc    pro  av  art   n   pro    av    adj   adj     n*

**7)** Whenever he gets a chance, he criticizes his other friends.

     *sc*    *pro*    *av*      *adj*      *n*     *pro*  *av*  *adj*  *conj*  *av*

**8)** <u>Unless he monopolizes every conversation</u>, he gets angry and sulks.

    *av*      —*v*—   *pp*    *pn*   *sc*  *pro*  *adv*   *av*  ——*v*——  *adj*    *n*

**9)** Remember to act (like Morris) <u>if you never want to have any friends</u>!

# Adverb Clauses: Exercise C

## Directions
Underline the adjective & adverb clauses in the sentences below. Circle the relative pronouns and the subordinating conjunctions. Above the clause write whether it's an adverb or adjective clause and what word in the main clause it modifies. This is what you will have to do on the assessment, so be sure you know what you're doing!

*adverb – borrowed*

**Example:** (Since) I did not have my math book, I borrowed one from Mary,

*adjective – Mary*

(who) is always prepared for class.

*adjective – class*

1) This class, (which) is considered to be the hardest in the school, will not seem so

*adverb –seem*

hard (after) it is finished.

*adjective – teacher*

2) My science teacher, (who) loves to build strange machines, and my math teacher,

*adjective – teacher*

(who) gets his kicks from solving difficult puzzles, will be the recipients of state

*adverb – be*

Teacher of the Year awards (because) they are such excellent teachers.

*adjective – girl*          *adverb – acted*

3) The girl (who) was sitting in the back row acted (as if) she had not heard the

teacher's instructions.

*adverb – become*

4) (When) I finally graduate from high school, the idea of going to college, (which)

*adjective – idea*

seems like a dream, will actually become a reality.

5) (Before) I left the auditorium, I asked the man (who) had given the speech

*adverb – asked*                              *adjective – man*

for an autograph.

6) I always get a souvenir (that) my little brother will like (whenever) I am on a trip.

*adjective – souvenir*              *adverb – get*

7) Students (who) read directions carefully usually do well (when) they are tested.

*adjective – students*                        *adverb – do*

8) (Whenever) I go on vacation, I like to buy something (that) reminds me of the place.

*adverb – like*                                        *adjective – something*

9) (Since) I had no homework, I decided to read a book (which) I had been wanting

*adverb – decided*                                    *adjective – book*

to read.

# Application & Enrichment

**Directions**

Parse all of the parts of speech that you know and put parentheses around the prepositional phrases. Use The Process Chart and your lesson notes if you need help.

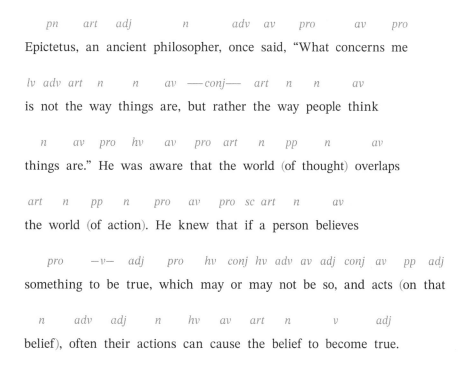

Next, write a paraphrase of the information in the paragraph. A good paraphrase should contain all of the ideas that are in the original paragraph. To be sure that you understand the main idea of each sentence and that you include all of the ideas, paraphrase the sentences individually in the spaces below. You may need to read the passage several times or look up unfamiliar words in the dictionary. You might even wish to discuss the sentences with your instructor. Once you understand what the sentence is saying, write it in your own words.

*Answers will vary. This formal language may be strange to your student. Help them to talk through the ideas in this passage so that they can write it in their own words.*

1) Epicetus, an ancient philosopher, once said, "What concerns me is not the way things are, but rather the way people think things are."

2) He was aware that the world of thought overlaps the world of action.

3) He knew that if a person believes something to be true, which may or may not be so, and acts on that belief, often their actions can cause the belief to become true.

# Adverb Clauses: Assessment

### Directions

The sentences below are short and choppy. Using adjective clauses or adverb clauses, combine the two sentences into one sentence.

Your sentence must:

- contain an adjective clause or an adverb clause, and

- contain all of the ideas in the original two sentences. You may change, add, or delete words if you want to.

*Answers will vary. These sentences are worth two points each: one for including an adjective clause or adverb clause, and one for including all of the ideas of the original two sentences. One possible solution is given.*

____ **1)** Henry Borsini is very tall. He is often asked to reach things on high shelves.

*2*      *Henry Borsini, who is very tall, is often asked to reach things on high shelves.*

____ **2)** I didn't have a warm coat. I borrowed one from a friend.

*2*      *Since I didn't have a warm coat, I borrowed one from a friend.*

____ **3)** I was almost asleep. I heard a sound that startled me awake.

*2*      *I was almost asleep when I heard a sound that startled me awake.*

____ **4)** Amy has never been outside the United States. She speaks German beautifully.

*2*      *Amy, who has never been outside the United States, speaks German beautifully.*

____ **5)** The Lawsons are our neighbors. They have gone to Hawaii for two weeks.

*2*      *The Lawsons, who are our neighbors, have gone to Hawaii for two weeks.*

____ **6)** That glass is chipped. It is dangerous.

*2*      *That glass, which is chipped, is dangerous.*

____ **7)** Ray searched for many days. He found the perfect gift.

*2*      *After Ray searched for many days, he found the perfect gift.*

____ **8)** Jane wanted to talk to that man. He was eating lunch in the same restaurant.

*2*      *Jane wanted to talk to that man who was eating lunch in the same restaurant.*

___**9)**  The twins had never seen a waterfall. Their uncle took them to Niagara Falls.

*2*        *The twins had never seen a waterfall before their uncle took them to Niagara Falls.*


___**10)**  The women couldn't walk very easily. They changed into flat-heeled shoes.

*2*        *The women couldn't walk very easily until they changed into flat-heeled shoes.*


*20*


## Directions

This assessment will check your understanding of both adjective and adverb clauses. There are twenty subordinate clauses in the story below.

On a separate sheet of paper:
Copy the entire subordinate clause. *(1 point)*
On the line below it, write whether it's an adjective clause or adverb clause. *(1 point)*
Circle the relative pronoun or subordinating conjunction. *(1 point)*
Write the word in the independent clause that the subordinate clause modifies. *(1 point)*
Try to number your clauses in the order they appear in the story.

*The solutions for this activity and the extra credit activity are found after Lesson 7.*

**Example:**        The old boxer who had retired from the ring was teaching the young fighter.

1)  (who) had retired from the ring

adjective clause - boxer


**11)**  Robert Browning, who was a poet of the Victorian period, wrote a poem about Childe Roland, a daring knight who set out on a dangerous quest for the Dark Tower. Many brave knights had been killed because they had searched for the Tower, but Roland was determined not to rest until he found it.

After Roland had searched for years, he came upon an old man who pointed the way to the Tower. Following the old man's directions, Roland found himself in a land which was horrible beyond belief. As he passed across the eerie wasteland, he saw all around him the signs of savage struggles that had taken place here in the past. Although Roland now felt doomed, he rode on. He saw sights that would have convinced the bravest of men to turn back. But Roland would not give up while he had the strength to continue.

Finally, when he had become discouraged, a large black bird swooped down over his head. As he watched it fly away, he saw in the distance the place which the old man had described to him. A dark tower loomed up before him as if a huge stone had arisen out of the valley. He felt like a sailor looking at a rocky shelf at the very moment that his ship crashes into it. While Roland paused to look, he heard ringing in his ears the names of all those who had died in the quest for the Tower. Then, on the hillsides, he saw in a sheet of flame the figures of the knights who had perished. In spite of the horror, Roland raised his horn to his lips and blew: "Childe Roland to the Dark Tower came!"


*80*

**Extra credit**

*Each correct answer is worth 3 points with each part of the answer accounting for 1 point. Add any extra credit points earned to the total score.*

In this story there is one appositive phrase, four infinitive phrases, and three participial phrases. Find as many as you can and write them on your paper. Be sure to tell what each item is as you write it down. What is the appositive restating? What job is each infinitive doing? What is each participial phrase modifying?

**Example:**        Bowser, my three-legged dog, falls over in a stiff wind.

my three-legged dog - appositive phrase - restates Bowser

*Add any extra credit points earned to the total score.*

$$\frac{\text{Total Points}}{100} \qquad \frac{80}{100} = 80\%$$

Extra Credit Points
24

# Noun Clauses

## Instructor Notes

With the experience your student has with subordinate clauses, infinitive and gerund phrases, and nouns and pronouns, they should have no trouble with this lesson. Remind them that the difference between these clauses and other subordinate clauses is the job that the clause is doing in the sentence. If it is doing the job of a noun (e.g., subject, direct object, indirect object, predicate nominative, or object of the preposition), then it is a noun clause.

The introductory word for these phrases has no special name. It should be parsed as either **pro** or **adv**, depending on the word. Instruction is provided demonstrating how to diagram these words.

*Diagramming solutions are found after Lesson 7.*

# Lesson 7: Noun Clauses

Congratulations—this is the last lesson in *Analytical Grammar Level 4: Phrases & Clauses*! After you finish it, you will have all of the grammar skills you need to be able to understand punctuation rules, the focus of *Analytical Grammar Level 5: Punctuation & Usage*. Let's finish strong with noun clauses!

## Noun clauses

A **noun clause** is a subordinate clause that is used as a noun in the sentence. A noun clause can do any of the jobs that a noun or pronoun can do: subject, direct object, indirect object, predicate nominative, or object of a preposition.

**Remember:** a clause has both a noun and a verb!

## Diagramming noun clauses

The noun clause goes on a stilt in the place where a single noun doing the same job would go, like gerund phrases and infinitive phrases doing the job of a noun. See the following examples:

**Example 1:**     Noun clause as subject

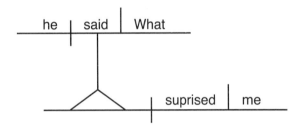

The noun clause *What he said* acts as the subject of the verb *surprised*.

**Example 2:**     Noun clause as predicate nominative

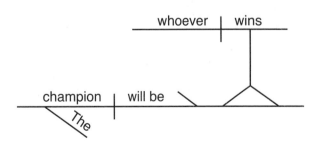

The noun clause *whoever wins* is the predicate nominative of the linking verb phrase *will be*.

**Example 3:**    Noun clause as direct object

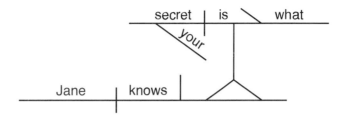

The noun clause *what your secret is* is the direct object of the verb *knows.*

**Example 4:**    Noun clause as indirect object

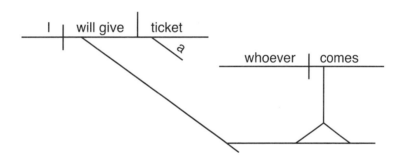

The noun clause *whoever comes* is the indirect object of the verb *give.*

**Example 5:**    Noun clause as object of the preposition

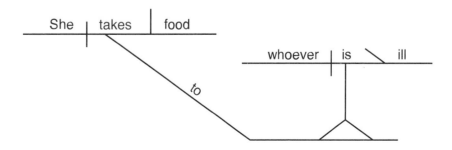

The noun clause *whoever is ill* is the object of the preposition *to.*

**Noun clauses** are usually introduced by the following pronouns:

| that | what | who | whom |
|------|------|------|------|
|      | whatever | whoever | whomever |

And sometimes by the following adverbs:

| where | when | why | how |
|-------|------|------|------|
| wherever | whenever | whyever | however |

Unlike relative pronouns or subordinating conjunctions, these introductory words have no special name of their own. Just parse them as **pro** or **adv**.

**Note:** Most of the time, the introductory word has some job to do in the clause; look at examples 1–5. Sometimes, however, the word **that** is used as an introductory word and it does nothing else in the clause at all. Its only function is to connect the subordinate clause to the main clause. Here's how you would diagram that:

pro    av    pro pro lv  adj

**Example 6:**   She thought <u>that I was sick</u>.

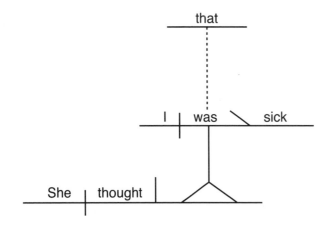

# Noun Clauses: Exercise A

**Directions**

Parse the sentences below and put the prepositional phrases in parentheses. Underline the noun clause. Diagram the sentence and then, under your diagram, write what job each noun clause is doing in the sentence.

    *pro   art   n     av    lv  art   adj     n*

**1)** <u>What the club wanted</u> was a haunted house.

       *Noun clause is the subject.*

    *adj    n     lv  pro pro  hv   adv  av   adv   pp     n*

**2)** His message was <u>that he would not be home</u> (for dinner).

       *Noun clause is the predicate nominative.*

    *art   n     av    pp   pro   art    n     av*

**3)** A guide pointed (to <u>where the picture was</u>).

       *Noun clause is the object of the preposition.*

    *art    n     av     pro    hv   av  art   n  art adj    n*

**4)** The teacher gave <u>whoever had read the story</u> a short quiz.

       *Noun clause is the indirect object.*

    *pn    adv    av  art  adj    n   pp     pro     pro   av*

**5)** Tammy always had a cheery hello (for <u>whomever she knew</u>).

       *Noun clause is the object of the preposition.*

    *pro     av    art  adj     n    pp    n     hv  av art   n*

**6)** <u>Whoever guesses the correct number</u> (of jellybeans) will win a prize!

       *Noun clause is the subject.*

    *art    n    pp  art adj    n    lv   pro   adv     av*

**7)** The outcome (of the whole thing) is <u>what really matters</u>.

       *Noun clause is the predicate nominative.*

    *art    n         av      pp  pro  adv    n    hv   av*

**8)** A beekeeper explained (to us) how honey is made.

      *Noun clause is the direct object.*


    *pro  pro  hv  adv    av     lv    adv      adj*

**9)** That she was not coming was quite obvious.

      *Noun clause is the subject.*


    *pro   lv      adj      pp   pro    av     adv      adv*

**10)** We were astonished (by what happened here yesterday).

      *Noun clause is the object of the preposition.*

# Noun Clauses: Exercise B

**Directions**

Underline every phrase (participial, gerund, infinitive, appositive) and every clause (adjective, adverb, noun) in each sentence. Identify each phrase or clause by writing above it what kind of phrase or clause it is and what job it is doing in the sentence. If it is modifying something, write what it is modifying.

*Adverb clause – modifies felt*        *Noun clause – direct object of felt*

**Example:**    When he heard Maria's speech, Mark felt that he should try harder.

*Noun clause –*    *Gerund phrase –*
*subject*    *predicate nominative*

**1)** What he does best is playing the piano.

*Adjective clause –*
*modifies man*

**2)** Mr. Allen is the man who taught us origami.

*Participial phrase –*    *Adverb clause –*
*modifies Jenny*    *modifies sat*

**3)** Screaming with fear, Jenny sat up suddenly when the tent collapsed.

*Appositive phrase –*    *Adverb clause –*
*restates family*    *modifies surprise*

**4)** My brother's family, our favorite relatives, surprises us whenever they arrive on time.

*Noun clause –*    *Infinitive –*    *Gerund phrase –*
*direct object*    *direct object*    *object of the preposition*

**5)** I could not understand what the directions said to do before entering the restricted area.

*Noun clause –*    *Participial phrase –*
*subject*    *modifies row*

**6)** Where we sat was the row of seats located near the exit.

*Adjective clause –*    *Infinitive phrase –*
*modifies Wolfman Jack*    *direct object*

**7)** Wolfman Jack, who was a disc jockey, loved to play old songs on

"The Midnight Special."

8) *Adjective clause –*
*modifies* oranges   *Adverb clause –*
*modifies* picked

8)   The oranges that we picked when we were in Florida were very juicy.

*Appositive phrase –*
*restates* Gene   *Noun clause –*
*object of the preposition*

9)   Gene, a thoughtful person, brought sandwiches for whoever was hungry.

*Participial phrase –*
*modifies* Horses   *Noun clause –*
*object of the preposition*

10)   Horses, considered stupid by many people, have strong feelings about where they go.

# Noun Clauses: Exercise C

**Directions**

Underline every phrase (participial, gerund, infinitive, appositive) and clause (adjective, adverb, noun). On a separate sheet of paper, write out each phrase or clause. Identify what kind of phrase or clause it is, and then write what job the phrase or clause is doing in the sentence. If it's modifying something, write what it's modifying.

1) Joe, <u>who was Mary's partner in the dance contest</u>, refused <u>to leave the dance floor</u> <u>when the judge tapped him on the shoulder</u>.

| | | |
|---|---|---|
| *who was Mary's partner in the dance contest* | *adjective clause* | *modifies* Joe |
| *to leave the dance floor* | *infinitive phrase* | *direct object* |
| *when the judge tapped him on the shoulder* | *adverb clause* | *modifies* refused |

2) Professor Watkins, <u>lecturing about the Amazon</u>,  absentmindedly left the room after the break <u>because he thought the class was over</u>.

| | | |
|---|---|---|
| *lecturing about the Amazon* | *participial phrase* | *modifies* Prof. Watkins |
| *because he thought the class was over* | *adverb clause* | *modifies* left |

3) The argument was all about <u>what Teresa had said</u> <u>when Jill told her a joke</u>.

| | | |
|---|---|---|
| *what Teresa had said* | *noun clause* | *object of the preposition* |
| *when Jill told her a joke* | *adverb clause* | *modifies* had said |

4) <u>Although they were already exhausted</u>, the first–string players stayed in the game.

| | | |
|---|---|---|
| *Although they were already exhausted* | *adverb clause* | *modifies* stayed |

5) Jason, <u>who is taller than Kyle</u>, thinks <u>that it would be funny</u> <u>if he played the part of Cinderella in the class play</u>.

| | | |
|---|---|---|
| *who is taller than Kyle* | *adjective clause* | *modifies* Jason |
| *that it would be funny* | *noun clause* | *direct object* |
| *if he played the part of Cinderella in the class play* | *adverb clause* | *modifies* funny |

6) <u>Saving the environment</u> has become an obsession for Tracy, <u>whom I was telling you about</u>.

| | | |
|---|---|---|
| *Saving the environment* | *gerund phrase* | *subject* |
| *whom I was telling you about* | *adjective clause* | *modifies* Tracy |

7) Karen, <u>burdened with a huge pile of books</u>, was staggering down the hall, and Kevin, <u>who is very thoughtful</u>, offered <u>to help her out</u>.

| | | |
|---|---|---|
| *burdened with a huge pile of books* | *participial phrase* | *modifies* Karen |
| *who is very thoughtful* | *adjective clause* | *modifies* Kevin |
| *to help her out* | *infinitive phrase* | *direct object* |

8) I turned around and only had a moment <u>to see a shadow</u>, <u>which I felt was that of a man</u>, <u>flitting past the open doorway</u>.

| | | |
|---|---|---|
| *to see a shadow* | *infinitive phrase* | *modifies* moment |
| *which I felt was that of a man* | *adjective clause* | *modifies* shadow |
| *flitting past the open doorway* | *participial phrase* | *modifies* shadow |

# Application & Enrichment

## Directions

The following is an excerpt from Dr. Martin Luther King, Jr.'s historic "I Have a Dream" speech, given on the steps of the Lincoln Memorial in 1963. Parse the words that you can in the passage below and put parentheses around the prepositional phrases. Then paraphrase it: read it and try to understand what is being said, then put it in your own words. It's okay if your sentences differ in number, length, or structure from the original passage. Write as many words as you need to include all of the ideas in the passage.

*Paraphrasing answers will vary*

    pro   av   ——v——   art   n    pp    n    lv    adj
"We refuse to believe the bank (of justice) is bankrupt...

    adv  lv  art  n   ——v——   n   art   n    pp   n   pp   adj      n
Now is the time to make justice a reality (for all) (of God's children).

    pro av art   n     adv
I have a dream today."

# Subordinate Clauses: Assessment

## Directions

The sentences in this exercise may include adjective, adverb, or noun clauses. On a separate sheet of paper, write out the entire subordinate clause in each sentence. Write what kind of subordinate clause it is. If it is a noun clause, write what job it is doing. If it is an adjective or adverb clause, write what word it modifies.

*Each correctly identified clause is worth three total points: one for identifying and writing the clause; one for identifying what kind of clause; and one for identifying the job or what is being modified.*

*The solutions to this portion of the assessment are found after this lesson.*

____ **1)** Leo claims that he knows judo.

____ **2)** Amy blushed when she read the letter.

____ **3)** The bait that worked best was shrimp.

____ **4)** Everyone who travels needs a map.

____ **5)** No one saw Diane before she got to practice.

____ **6)** The wolf attacked because it was trapped.

____ **7)** The robot will do whatever you ask.

____ **8)** The test, which was quite hard, lasted one hour.

____ **9)** We went to the circus when it came to town.

____ **10)** What I like best is talking on the phone with friends.

____ **11)** The champion beat whomever he fought.

____ **12)** A person who designs buildings is an architect.

____ **13)** Kenny Loggins is the one who plays guitar.

____ **14)** Whoever returns the stolen jewels will get a reward.

____ **15)** The dog followed John wherever he went.

____ **16)** Although she prefers hockey, Grace plays center on the basketball team.

____ **17)** Many people watch television because they are bored.

____ **18)** We could see the lake from where we stood.

____ **19)** Slavery was what divided the country.

____ **20)** Radar, which locates distant objects, is used to track spacecraft.

*60*

**Directions**

Write the clauses (adjective, adverb, or noun) and phrases (participial, gerund, infinitive, or appositive) that you find on the lines provided below each sentence. The number of phrases or clauses per sentence is provided. Identify what kind of clause or phrase it is. Be alert–one of the answers is a single word!

Be sure to copy out the entire phrase or clause if possible! (If you can't fit the entire phrase or clause on the line provided, write the first word, then use an ellipsis in brackets like this: [...], and then write the last word. See the example for what this looks like.)

These sentences are from *The Hound of the Baskervilles* by Sir Arthur Conan Doyle, which is one of the most famous Sherlock Holmes mysteries.

*Note: Use your own discretion as to where phrases and clauses begin and end. For example, in sentence 1, your student might write* to be a large black calf passing at the head of the drive *as one complete infinitive phrase. That's okay; count it correct as long as they then identify* passing at the head of the drive *as a participial phrase as well. Clauses and phrases can be nested within each other as writing gets more complex.*

**Examples:**     On the night of Sir Charles's death, Barrymore the butler, who made the discovery, sent Perkins the groom on horseback to me. (three phrases/clauses)

1) the butter                    appositive phrase

2) who[...]discovery        adjective clause

3) the groom                   appositive phrase

21) I whisked round and had just time to catch a glimpse of something which I took to be a large black calf passing at the head of the drive. (four phrases/clauses)

  $\frac{\quad}{2}$ #1  *to catch a glimpse of something*                    *infinitive phrase*

  $\frac{\quad}{2}$ #2  *which I took to be a large black calf*              *adjective clause*

  $\frac{\quad}{2}$ #3  *to be a large black calf*                                      *infinitive phrase*

  $\frac{\quad}{2}$ #4  *passing at the head of the drive*                      *participial phrase*

22) A hound it was, an enormous coal-black hound, but not such a hound as mortal eyes have ever seen. (two phrases/clauses)

  $\frac{\quad}{2}$ #1  *an enormous coal-black hound*                        *appositive phrase*

  $\frac{\quad}{2}$ #2  *as mortal eyes have ever seen*                          *adverb clause*

**23)** With long bounds the huge black creature was leaping down the track, following hard upon the footsteps of our friend. (one phrase/clause)

$\frac{\quad}{2}$ **#1** _following hard upon the footsteps of our friend_      _participial phrase_

**24)** Never have I seen a man run as Holmes ran that night. (one phrase/clause)

$\frac{\quad}{2}$ **#1** _as Holmes ran that night_      _adverb clause_

**25)** "There is a delightful freshness about you, Watson, which makes it a pleasure to exercise any small powers which I possess at your expense." (four phrases/clauses)

$\frac{\quad}{2}$ **#1** _Watson_      _appositive_

$\frac{\quad}{2}$ **#2** _which makes it a pleasure_      _adjective clause_

$\frac{\quad}{2}$ **#3** _to exercise any small powers_      _infinitive phrase_

$\frac{\quad}{2}$ **#4** _which I possess_      _adjective clause_

$\overline{\overline{\quad}}$
_24_

**Extra credit**

This is the last diagram you will be asked to create in *Analytical Grammar*! (Although we do hope you will find those skills useful in polishing your writing skills and in determining meaning in complex sentences.) For five extra credit points, diagram the following sentence:

How much wood would a woodchuck chuck if a woodchuck could chuck wood?

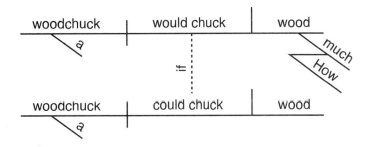

*Start with five possible points and deduct one point for each error. Add any extra credit points earned to the total score.*

══ *Total Points*     $\dfrac{67}{84} = 80\%$
84

══ *Extra Credit Points*
5

**Reinforcing Skills**

Congratulations on completing Level 4! At this point, it's important to reinforce the parsing and diagramming skills your student learned in these lessons so they aren't forgotten. Your student will use these grammar skills as they learn about punctuation and usage in Level 5.

The student worktext includes ten reinforcement exercises and answer keys that will keep your student's parsing, diagramming, and paraphrasing skills sharp. These exercises include material from a wide variety of books, poems, and stories. While completing these exercises, they might find something they would love to read!

Students should complete, then correct, each exercise on their own. Assign one exercise every other week. Remind your student to use The Process Chart and the notes if they help. If these skills are reinforced periodically, your student will be well-prepared when it's time to start Level 5.

## Lesson 1: Participial Phrases

### Exercise A

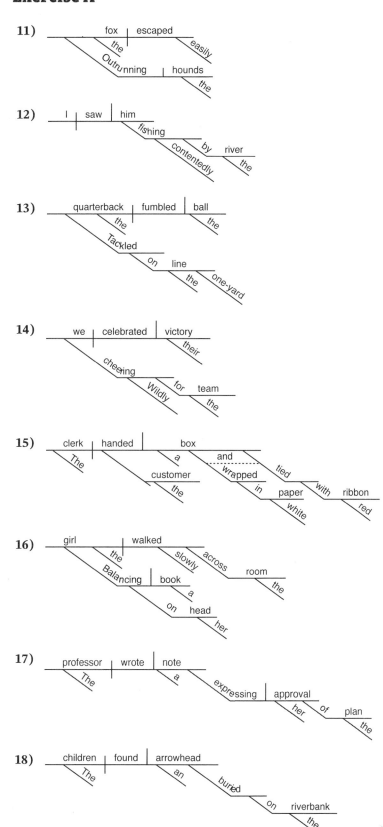

# Exercise B

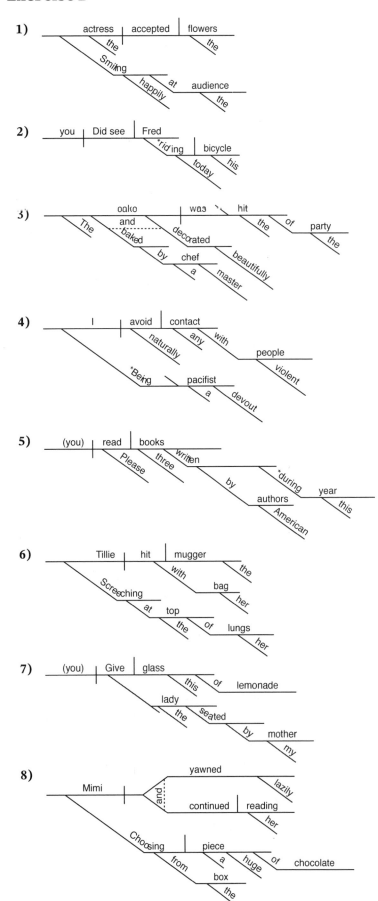

# Exercise C

1)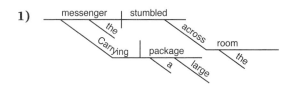

2)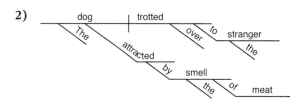

3)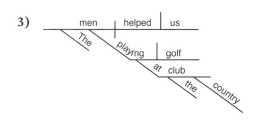

4)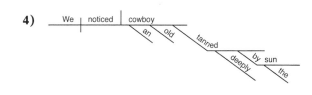

5)

6)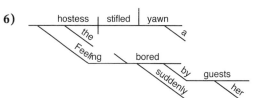

7)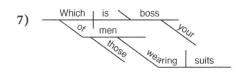

8)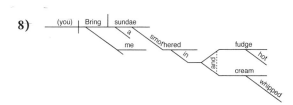

9)

10)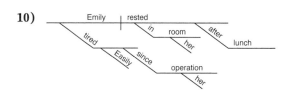

## Assessment

Although prepositional phrases are usually only worth one point, for this lesson, those with compound objects will be worth more as shown.

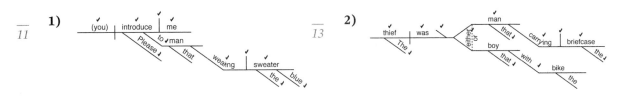

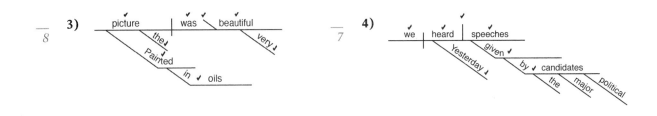

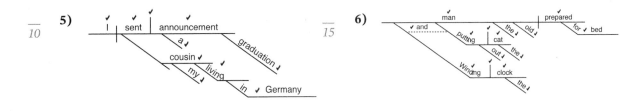

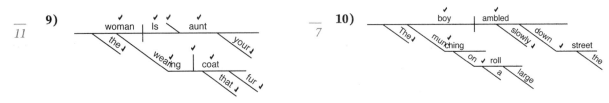

### Diagrams

*Transfer diagraming points to lesson assessment.*

═══ *Total Points*
   *99*

## Lesson 2: Gerund Phrases

### Exercise A

8)

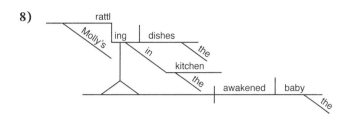

9)

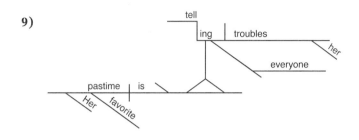

10)

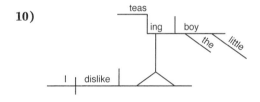

## Exercise B

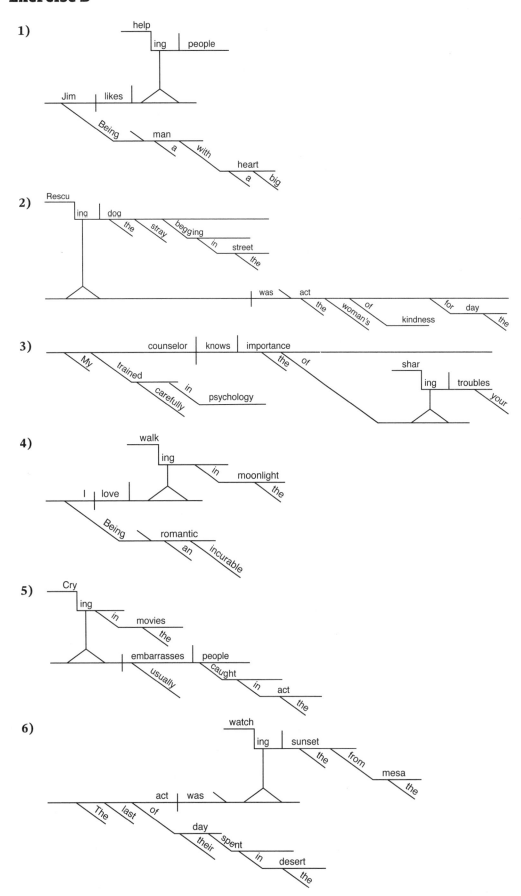

## Exercise C

1)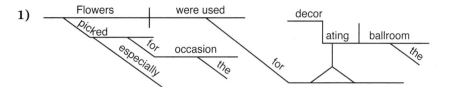

2)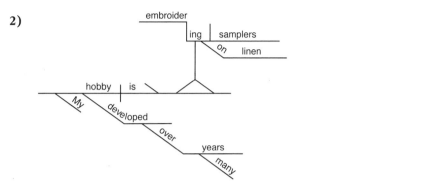

3)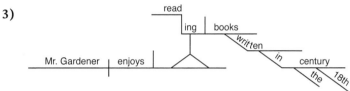

4)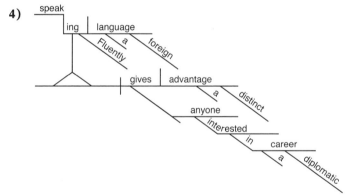

5)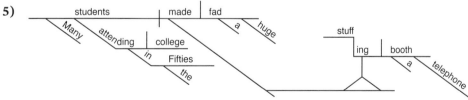

6)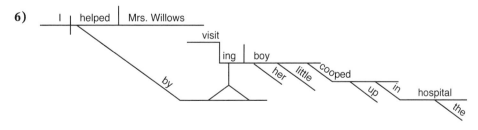

## Assessment

Although prepositional phrases are usually only worth one point, for this lesson, those with compound objects will be worth more as shown.

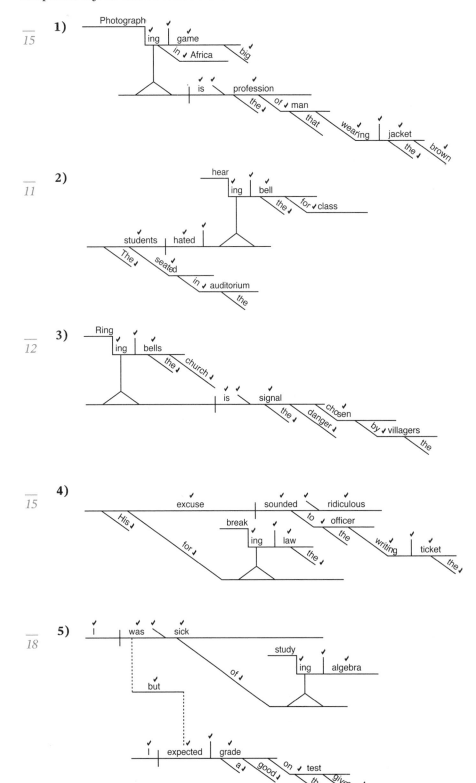

$\overline{15}$ **1)**

$\overline{11}$ **2)**

$\overline{12}$ **3)**

$\overline{15}$ **4)**

$\overline{18}$ **5)**

## Assessment

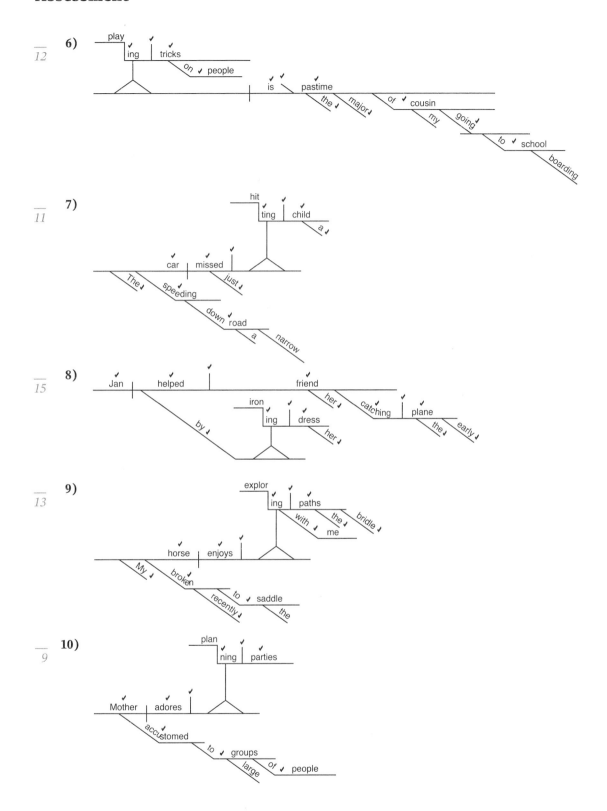

6)
$\overline{12}$

7)
$\overline{11}$

8)
$\overline{15}$

9)
$\overline{13}$

10)
$9$

## Diagrams

*Transfer diagraming points to lesson assessment.*

═══ *Total Points*
*131*

## Lesson 3: Infinitive Phrases

### Exercise A

6)

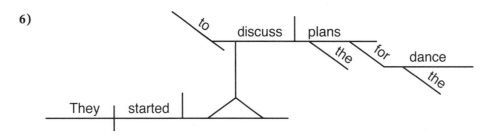

7)

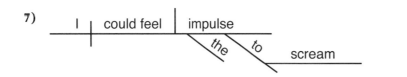

8)

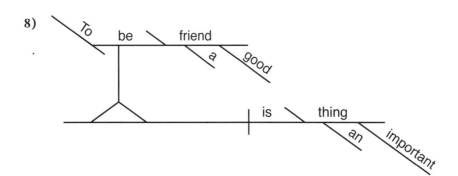

9)

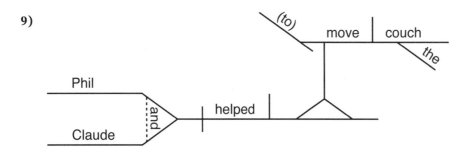

10)

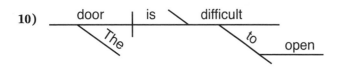

## Exercise B

1)

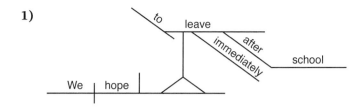

2)

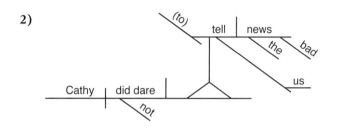

3)

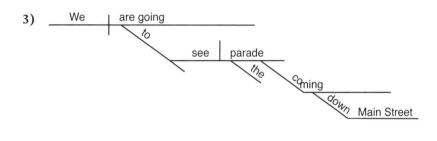

4)

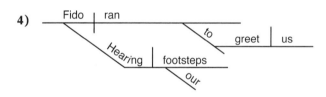

5)

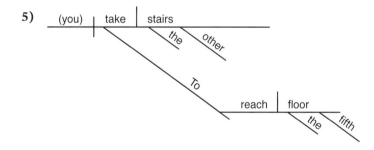

## Exercise B

**6)**

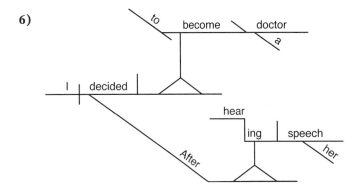

**7)**

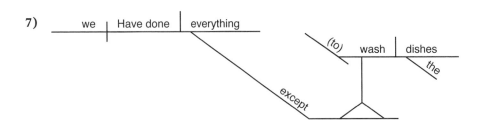

**8)**

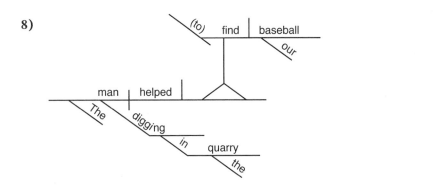

**9)**

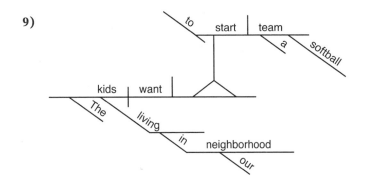

**10)**

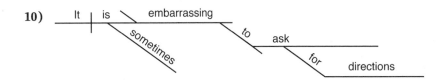

## Exercise C

1)

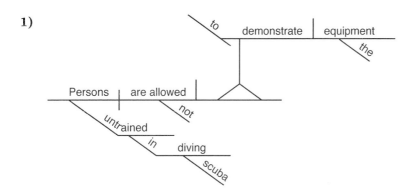

2)

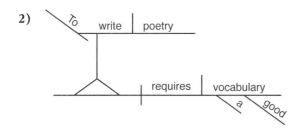

3)

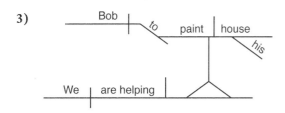

4)

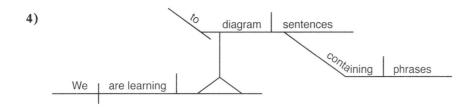

5)

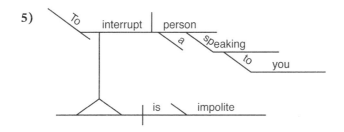

## Exercise C

6)

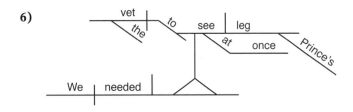

7)

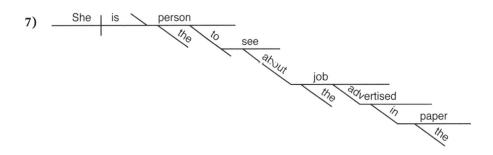

8)

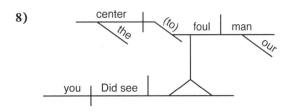

9)

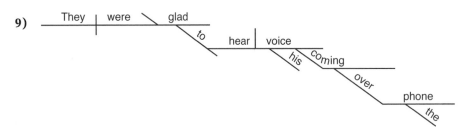

10)

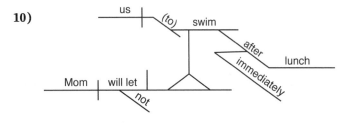

## Assessment

Although prepositional phrases are usually only worth one point, for this lesson, those with compound objects will be worth more as shown.

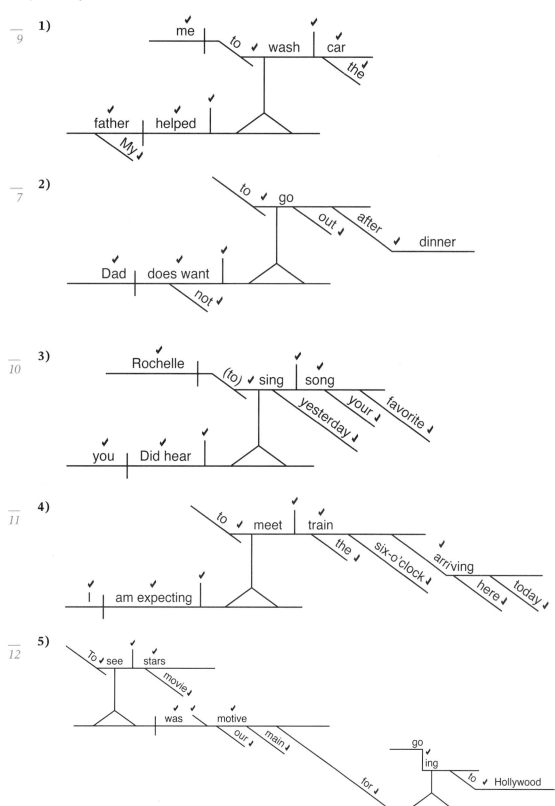

$\frac{}{9}$ **6)**

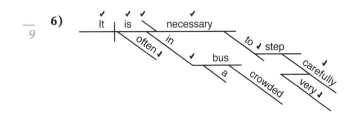

$\frac{}{14}$ **7)**

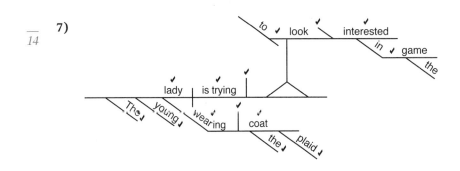

$\frac{}{10}$ **8)**

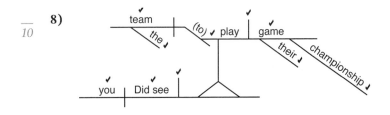

$\frac{}{7}$ **9)**

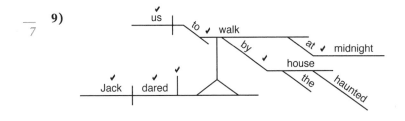

$\frac{}{15}$ **10)**

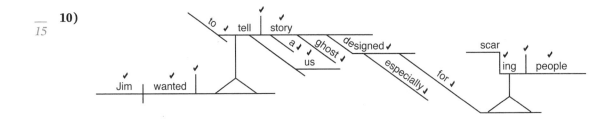

## Diagrams

*Transfer diagraming points to lesson assessment.*

$\overline{\overline{\phantom{===}}}$ *Total Points*

*104*

## Lesson 4: Appositive Phrases

### Exercise B

**4)**

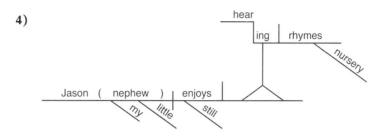

**5)**

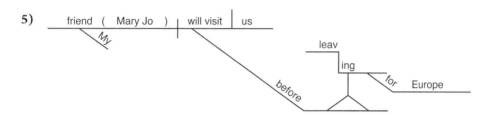

**6)**

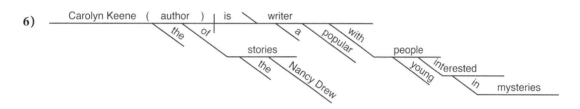

**7)**

## Exercise C

1)

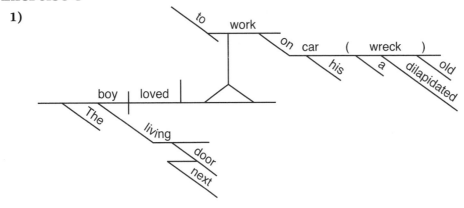

2)

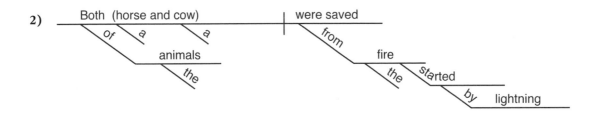

3)

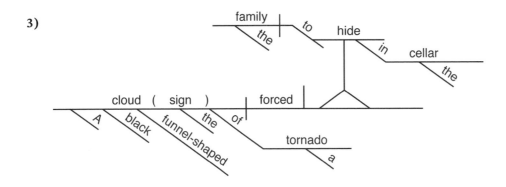

## Assessment

Although prepositional phrases are usually only worth one point, for this lesson, those with compound objects will be worth more as shown.

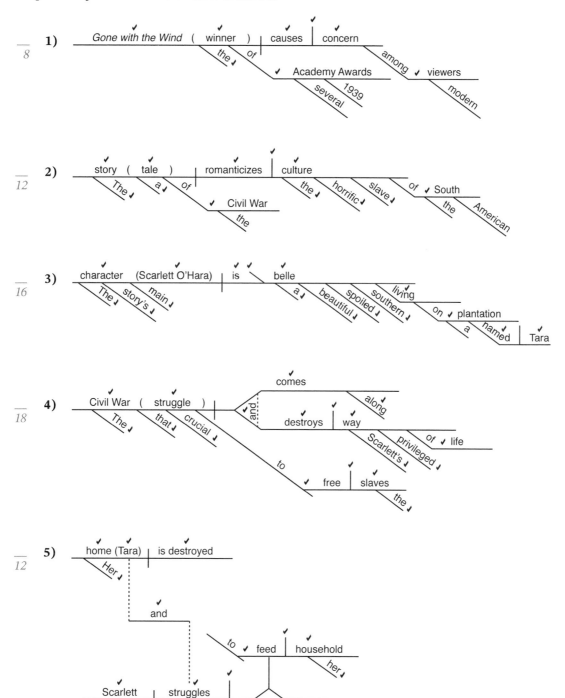

1) —8—

2) —12—

3) —16—

4) —18—

5) —12—

## Diagrams

*Transfer diagraming points to lesson assessment.*

Total Points
66

## Lesson 5: Adjective Clauses

### Exercise B

**1)**

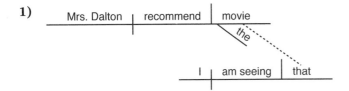

**2)**

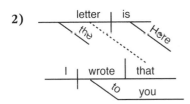

**3)**

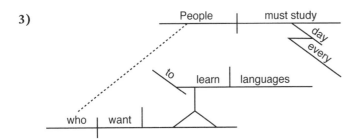

**4)**

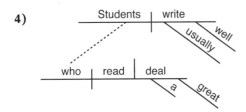

**5)**

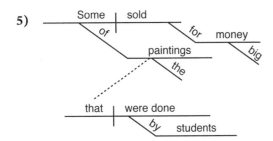

## Exercise B

6)

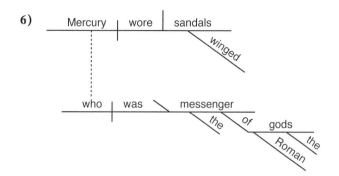

7)

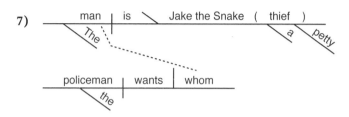

8)

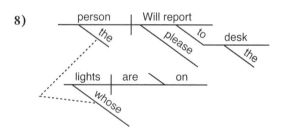

9)

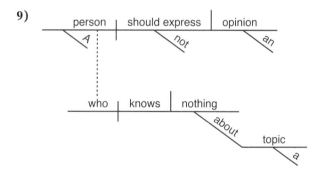

10)

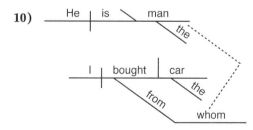

## Exercise C

Although prepositional phrases are usually only worth one point, for this lesson, those with compound objects will be worth more as shown.

**1)**
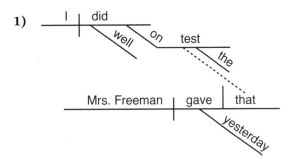

**2)**
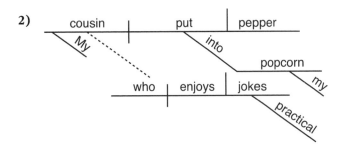

**3)**
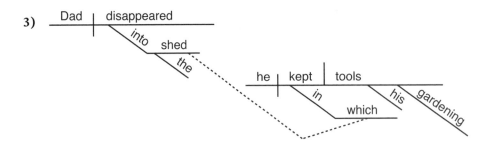

**4)**
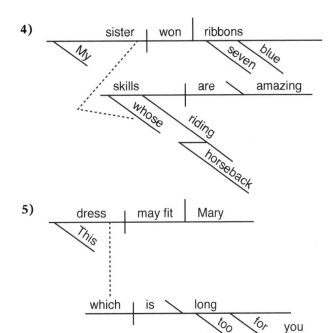

**5)**

## Assessment

**1)**

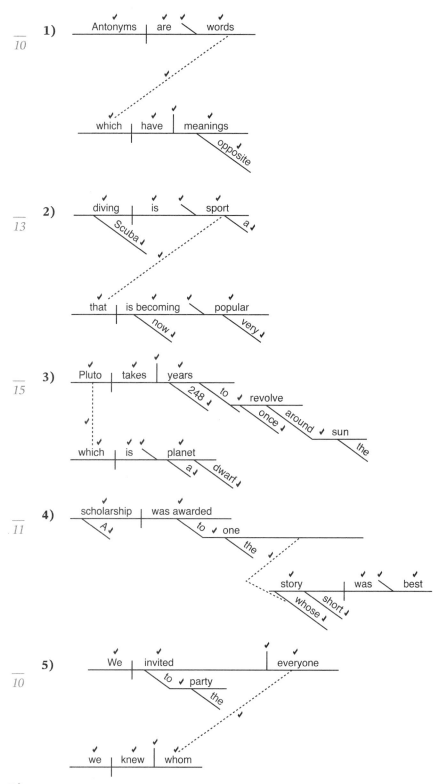

**2)**

**3)**

**4)**

**5)**

## Diagrams

*Transfer diagraming points to lesson assessment.*

*Total Points*
*59*

## Lesson 6: Adverb Clauses

### Exercise A

1)

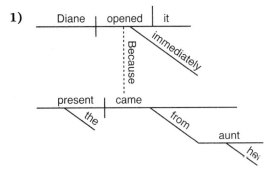

2)

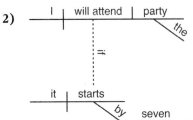

3)

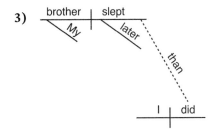

4)

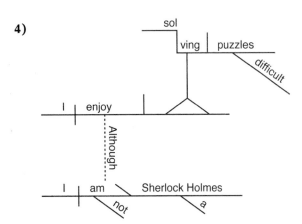

5)

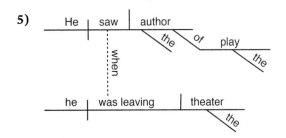

## Exercise A

**6)**

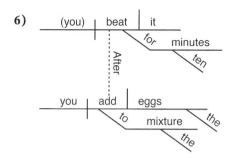

**7)**

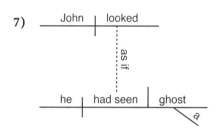

**8)**

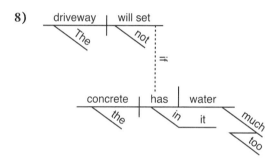

**9)**

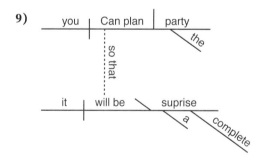

**10)**

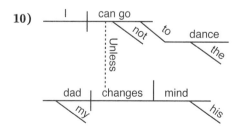

## Exercise B

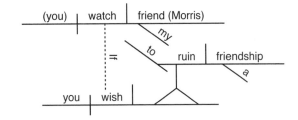

**1)**

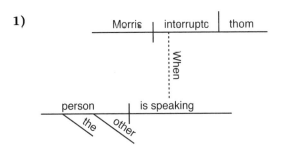

**2)**

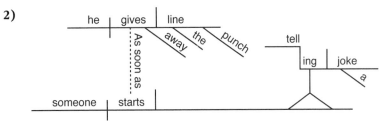

**3)**

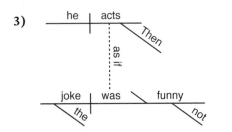

**4)**

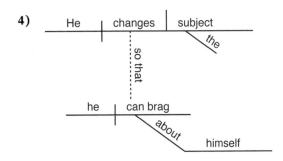

## Exercise B

5)
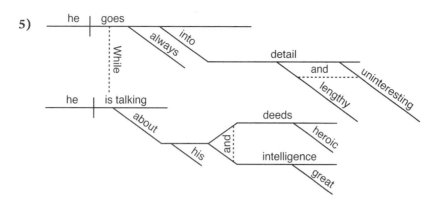

6)
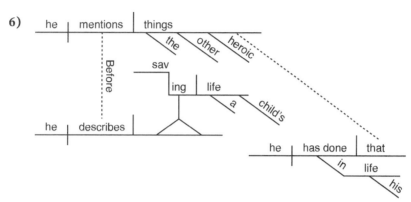

7)
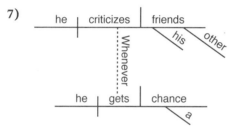

8)
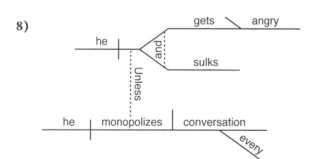

9)
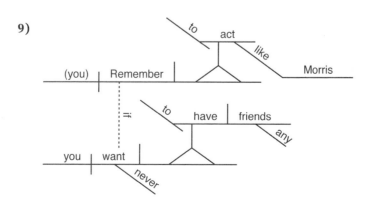

## Assessment

*Each of these answers is worth four points: one for identifying the subordinate clause; one for identifying whether it is an adjective clause or adverb clause; one for circling the relative pronoun or subordinating conjunction; and one for identifying the word that the clause is modifying.*

___ **1)** (who) was a poet of the Victorian period     adjective clause     Robert Browning
4

___ **2)** (who) set out on a dangerous quest for the Dark Tower     adjective clause     knight
4

___ **3)** (because) they had searched for the Tower     adverb clause     (had been) killed
4

___ **4)** (until) he found it     adverb clause     (to) rest
4

___ **5)** (After) Roland had searched for years     adverb clause     came
4

___ **6)** (who) pointed the way to the Tower     adjective clause     man
4

___ **7)** (which) was horrible beyond belief     adjective clause     land
4

___ **8)** (As) he passed across the eerie wasteland     adverb clause     saw
4

___ **9)** (that) had taken place here in the past     adjective clause     struggles
4

___ **10)** (Although) Roland now felt doomed     adverb clause     rode
4

___ **11)** (that) would have convinced the bravest of men to turn back     adjective clause     sights
4

___ **12)** (while) he had strength to continue     adverb clause     (would) give
4

___ **13)** (when) he had become discouraged     adverb clause     swooped
4

___ **14)** (As) he watched it fly away     adverb clause     saw
4

___ **15)** (which) the old man had described to him     adjective clause     place
4

___ **16)** (as if) a huge stone had arisen out of the valley     adverb clause     loomed
4

___ **17)** (that) his ship crashes into it     adjective clause     moment
4

___**18)** (While) *Roland paused to look*       *adverb clause*       *heard*
 4

___**19)** (who) *had died in their quest for the Tower*       *adjective clause*       *those*
 4

___**20)** (who) *had perished*       *adjective clause*       *knights*
 4

══
80

*Extra credit solutions:*

*There are eight correct responses below worth three points each: one point for correctly saying what kind of phrase it is, one for copying out the entire phrase correctly, and one point for correctly identifying what it restates, modifies, or what job it does in the sentence. They can get partial credit if they have some parts correct but not others. In all, this extra credit is worth 24 points!*

| | | |
|---|---|---|
| *appositive phrase* | a daring knight | *restates* Childe Roland |
| *infinitive phrase* | (not) to rest | *modifier* |
| *infinitive phrase* | to turn back | *modifier* |
| *infinitive phrase* | to continue | *modifier* |
| *infinitive phrase* | to look | *modifier* |
| *participial phrase* | following the old man's directions | *modifies* Roland |
| *participial phrase* | looking at a rocky shelf | *modifies* sailor |
| *participial phrase* | ringing in his ears | *modifies* names |

══
24

## Lesson 7: Noun Clauses

### Exercise A

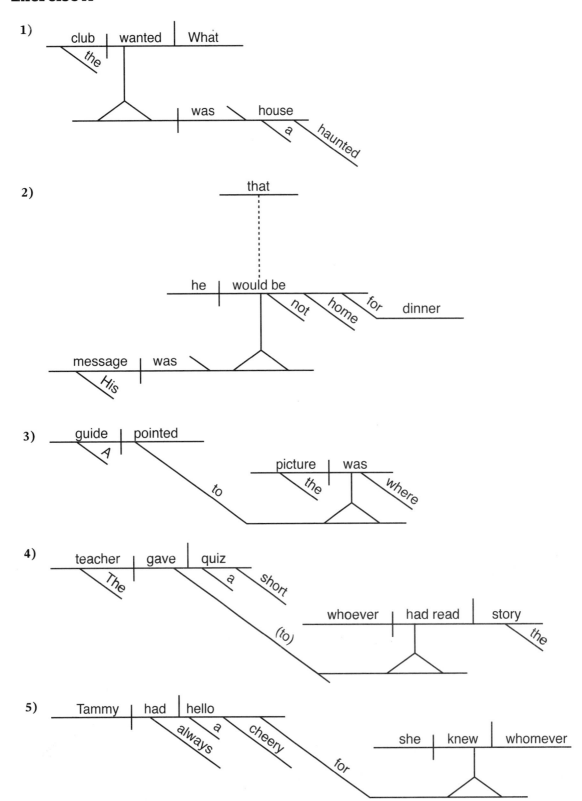

6)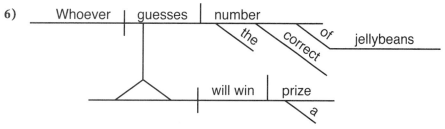

7)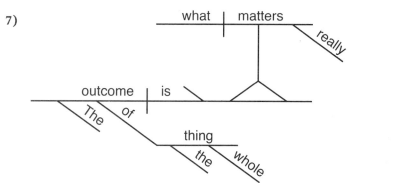

8)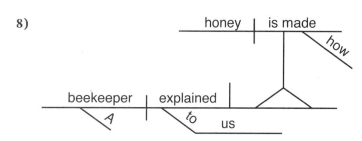

9)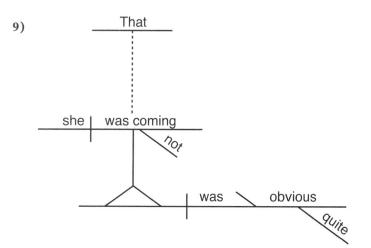

10)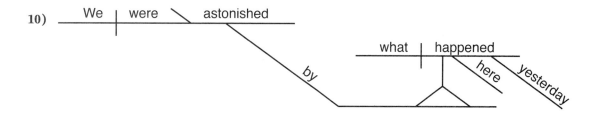

## Assessment

*Each correctly identified clause is worth three total points: one for identifying and writing the clause; one for identifying what kind of clause; and one for identifying the job or what is being modified.*

| | | | |
|---|---|---|---|
| __3__ | **1)** *that he knows judo* | *noun clause* | *direct object* |
| __3__ | **2)** *when she read the letter* | *adverb clause* | *modifies* blushed |
| __3__ | **3)** *that worked best* | *adjective clause* | *modifies* bait |
| __3__ | **4)** *who travels* | *adjective clause* | *modifies* Everyone |
| __3__ | **5)** *before she got to practice* | *adverb clause* | *modifies* saw |
| __3__ | **6)** *because it was trapped* | *adverb clause* | *modifies* attacked |
| __3__ | **7)** *whatever you ask* | *noun clause* | *direct object* |
| __3__ | **8)** *which was quite hard* | *adjective clause* | *modifies* test |
| __3__ | **9)** *when it came to town* | *adverb clause* | *modifies* went |
| __3__ | **10)** *What I like best* | *noun clause* | *subject* |
| __3__ | **11)** *whomever he fought* | *noun clause* | *direct object* |
| __3__ | **12)** *who designs buildings* | *adjective clause* | *modifies* person |
| __3__ | **13)** *who plays guitar* | *adjective clause* | *modifies* one |
| __3__ | **14)** *Whoever returns the stolen jewels* | *noun clause* | *subject* |
| __3__ | **15)** *wherever he went* | *adverb clause* | *modifies* followed |
| __3__ | **16)** *Although she prefers hockey* | *adverb clause* | *modifies* plays |
| __3__ | **17)** *because they are bored* | *adverb clause* | *modifies* watch |
| __3__ | **18)** *where we stood* | *noun clause* | *object of the preposition* |
| __3__ | **19)** *what divided the country* | *noun clause* | *predicate nominative* |
| __3__ | **20)** *which locates distant objects* | *adjective clause* | *modifies* radar |

___
*60*

# Index

Concepts are listed by lesson number.

*Indicates item is found in Application & Enrichment activity

# Bibliography

Florey, Kitty Burns. Sister Bernadette's Barking Dog: The Quirky History and Lost Art of Diagramming Sentences. Orlando, FL: Harcourt, 2007.

Garner, Bryan A. Garner's Modern English Usage. Oxford: Oxford University Press, 2016.

Garner, Bryan A. The Chicago Guide to Grammar, Usage, and Punctuation. Chicago, IL: The University of Chicago Press, 2016.

Truss, Lynne. Eats, Shoots & Leaves: The Zero Tolerance Approach to Punctuation. London: Fourth Estate, 2009.